The
*Invisible
Garden*

The
Invisible
Garden

Dorothy Sucher

Woodcuts by Mary Azarian

COUNTERPOINT
NEW YORK

Library of Congress Cataloging-in-Publication Data
Sucher, Dorothy
    The invisible garden / Dorothy Sucher.
       p. cm.
    ISBN 1-58243-127-2
    1. Gardening–Vermont Anecdotes. 2. Sucher, Dorothy.
I. Title
SB 455.S88   1999
635'.09743—dc21   99-16301
                                      CIP

DHSB 02 03 04 10 9 8 7 6 5

Book and jacket design by Amy Evans McClure

Printed in the United States of America on acid-free paper that meets the American National Standards Institute Z39-48 Standard.

COUNTERPOINT
387 Park Avenue South
New York, NY 10016-8810

Counterpoint is a member of the Perseus Books Group.

To Anita Landa and Mary Belenky,
who welcomed me to Vermont

Contents

Acknowledgments

My appreciation goes to Joyce Johnson for several help-ful conversations and astute comments, and to Charles Johnson for generously sharing his vast knowledge of Vermont trees and other growing things.

I thank the members of the Greenbelt Writers Group, and also Bob and Mary Belenky, Dan Chodorkoff, Blythe and Evans Clinchy, Susan Thomas, and Eileen Peterson for their encouragement and warm support.

As for my husband, Joe Sucher, there is no way to thank him adequately for his help. He is my first, best, and dearest reader.

I have mentioned several books in passing, including Henry W. Art's *A Garden of Wildflowers: 101 Native Species and How to Grow Them* (Storey Communications, 1986); Janet Kauffman's *Places in the World a Woman Could Walk* (Graywolf Press, 1996); and Tim Matson's *Earth Ponds: The Country Pond Maker's Guide* (Countryman Press, Vermont, 1991). Several of Gertrude Jekyll's gardening books have been reprinted fairly recently, including *Wall, Water, and Woodland Gardens* (Antique Collectors' Club, 1994).

Now out of print, alas, but occasionally to be found in used book stores is Norman Taylor's wonderfully detailed and inclusive *Encyclopedia of Gardening* (Houghton Mifflin, 1948). As for the multivolume children's encyclopedia *The Book of Knowledge,* the edition (now lost) I devoured as a child in the 1940s was ancient even then, a tattered library discard with loose covers that nonetheless welcomed me into a world of wonders I still inhabit.

The
Invisible
Garden

Prologue

When my husband and I bought our old blue farmhouse in Vermont, I had no idea I would become a gardener there. But that was how it turned out. For me, as for so many others, gardening became the way I could connect most intensely with nature and come to know its rhythms, its gifts, and its complications. It was also a way of coming to know myself better.

Maybe my becoming a gardener was inevitable, for gardening is an obsession among my Vermont community of friends. Most of us do other kinds of work as well, work we think of as more "real," but gardens serve as our common denominator; when we meet, it is of nurserymen and perennials and manure and stone that we most often speak.

The short Vermont growing season has much to do with our gardening mania. After the long, frozen, cabin-feverish Vermont winter has segued into endless, dreary mud season, when everyone who can afford it takes off for other climes, spring comes in a surge. We rush to meet it as if flinging ourselves into a love affair that is doomed to be short. Spring peepers shrill their mating cries as greenness bursts from the earth, the scents of lilac and apple blossom commandeer the breeze, and suddenly new sprouts, seedlings, and weeds shoot up everywhere you look—almost as you look. Cleanup, planting, and weeding demand to be done instantly, just when the blackflies are at their absolute worst.

We plunge into the annual ritual, complaining of our aching bones and bemoaning the fact that we have no time for our real work. Grime takes up permanent residence under our nails. We count our blackfly bites and finger the bee-keeping veils at the general store and weigh the merits and demerits of Skin-so-Soft (greasy, smells good, said to be non-toxic but you have to keep smearing it on every hour) versus hardcore Deet (keeps the bugs off but might give you cancer).

If the season also brings serious deadlines at our real work, we feel torn. We try to be in two places at once, like working mothers with young children. Caretakers' guilt assails us, for our charges will languish and sulk if we neglect them, or run wild and mingle with the wrong companions. We are needed and we know it.

Gardens are living things, as unique as children and issuing from their own kind of labor. Once we have brought them forth, deep and intimate bonds develop between the maker and the garden. We come to know the nature of our soil, which can vary subtly from place to place; we learn to recognize the sheltered microclimates where we can tuck the more tender plants, trusting that they will thrive. We ponder mysteries, like why the monarda that spreads with such abandon in our wildflower meadow languishes in the garden down the road, or why the pink peony that annually bursts the bonds of our neighbor's peony hoop barely survives in our sunniest bed once we have acquired a specimen of exactly the same variety.

The gardens in this book are real, and therefore imperfect—unlike the illustrations in many gardening books. I'm not referring just to photographs of stately gardens maintained by great wealth and a large staff of gardeners, which really do look like their pictures—and why shouldn't they?—but to quite a few of the looser, more naturalistic country and suburban gardens pictured in gardening magazines.

Only this year I was shocked to learn that some of the glossy, picture-book gardens I've studied so longingly were practically trucked in for the photographer's visit, like exhibits set up in a garden show in a downtown coliseum. I don't mean meticulous weeding and a few new plants tucked here and there into bare spots. I mean whole borders dug up and replanted with mature specimens grown somewhere else. I mean publicists running around plopping down rustic furniture and antique beehives and birdhouses to create a "garden" that not only no longer exists but never did exist.

What has all this to do with the exasperating, sweaty grappling with nature that is gardening? About as much as watching television has to do with actually living. The gardens in this book may be modest, amateurish, and messy in comparison, but one thing is certain: they were not trucked in for the occasion.

Gardens give their owners so much joy and discontent that sometimes they seem to be a metaphor for life. There is more to them than meets the eye; all sorts of memories and emotions cling to them. The clump of lemon lilies recalls the day it mysteriously appeared on the doorstep, left by an anonymous caller; the delicate, finely-cut ferns of asparagus bring to mind the memory of a beloved grandfather; the sumptuous globe of a peony, bending under its own weight, serves as a reminder of a child's wonder at what seemed to be drops of blood on the white petals. I think of this complex of conscious and unconscious associations as an "invisible garden" that each of us, gardeners and garden visitors alike, carries around. These associations remain dormant until the plants we happen to be looking at reawaken them. Then old, half-forgotten feelings wash over us, perhaps joy and pleasure, perhaps loss and pain. We can never know in advance how walking through a garden will make us feel. Sometimes the fresh perceptions of childhood come back to us for a few glorious moments. Sometimes, seemingly for no reason at all, we become sad. Always it is the invisible garden that gives the visible garden its deepest meaning.

As we work around the garden we do our best, within the bounds of our human limitations, to provide what is needed. We water and fertilize, pinch and prune, stake and weed; or at least we try. The garden gives us back so much that at times it's hard not to sense a consciousness out there, a living earth-spirit that appreciates our efforts and reaches out to heal us when we are troubled. In certain special places, that earth-spirit seems to resonate with greater intensity; I have written about a few of these in the essays "Bones of the Earth" and "The Spring."

In a sense this book is more about gardeners than gardens. To me, visiting a private garden, no matter how lovely, is an incomplete experience without meeting the gardener. Of all the gardens I describe, the one that attracted the most visitors was the garden created by the late herbalist Adele Dawson, who passed on her love of gardening to me; the real magnet was her personality. Believed by some to be a witch, Adele brought warmth and laughter and good cooking, as well as healing, into the lives of the many friends and students who were drawn into her orbit, right up to the end of her long life.

When I write of my own garden, I use the term in its broadest sense to include the thirty acres we acquired rather late in life—far more land than we ever dreamed of owning. Most of it is undeveloped, and little by little I have been getting to know it. Some of it I have changed, and the process of doing so—digging a pond, clearing a path, and making or trying to make gardens— has been for me an ongoing adventure as well as a process of discovery.

Writing this book has brought me some surprises. When I started to write about our daffodil border, the piece turned into a reminiscence of my late gardener, Wanda Mayhew, whose posthumous gift it was. Wanda's spirit will always be the "invisible" aspect of that part of my garden, and every spring when the daffodils bloom, especially the white ones that are the same color as her hair, a beloved friend comes back to me for a brief season.

Writing about the building of our pond proved to be unexpectedly difficult. I couldn't seem to get started until I remembered that we'd built the pond in the aftermath of my mother's death. Then it hit me that the pond and my mother were powerfully connected in my mind. Only then did the writing begin to flow.

Nobody who sees my pond would know this, of course. I was hardly conscious of it myself until I began to write. Similarly, other people have their hidden connections to the landscapes that surround them, and these I've tried to explore and celebrate.

In addition to the gardeners, both private and professional, about whom I have written, certain other people make an appearance here because they, too, are part of garden-making. There is no one word that includes bulldozer and backhoe operators, stonemasons, carpenters, pond builders, nurserymen, hardware store clerks, tree specialists, sawmill operators, and the bringers of loads of topsoil and manure—not to mention those who do a little of everything. They are often skilled and knowledgeable folk, and sometimes they are artists. They make up the gardener's support system, and my dealings with them have taught me that more is involved than a simple exchange of money for services. These relationships, sometimes short and sometimes lasting, bring the pleasures of sociability to the solitary pursuit of gardening.

When we garden, whether we realize it or not, we bring to bear our previous life experiences, our memories of childhood and travel, our family relations, our reading, our dreams and aspirations, our moral standards and character flaws, our sensuality and grandiosity and spirituality. All of these are part of the invisible garden.

The Stream

The blue farmhouse had a neglected, almost derelict air. It sat beside the road in a semicircular clearing behind which rose a wooded hill. As I picked my way to the door, between the sodden mattresses and smashed cardboard cartons that lay decomposing in the mud, I asked myself what I was doing there. I'd come to Vermont to spend a quiet country weekend, and now I was in the clutches of a realtor intent on showing me every property on the market. Why had I thought that looking at houses would be a fun way to spend a rainy day?

Inside, the house was dank and chill. The living room was small, the wallpaper hung in shreds, and the four bedrooms were more than my husband and I would ever need now that our children were grown. Maybe with a fire in the woodstove and a little fixing up the place wouldn't be too bad; I didn't care. All I wanted was to go back to the inn and take a nap.

I shook my head and we left the house. The realtor said, "The stream is across the road."

"Stream?" Now that I listened, I could hear the rushing of the water. I'd told the realtor I had to have a stream. Might as well ask for perfection, I'd thought, the fulfillment of every fantasy. Why not? I was only playing at house-hunting, passing through the area and visiting an old friend. Passing time.

We crossed the road and pushed our way through a thick growth of ferns that came up to my waist. As we pressed forward, the rushing sound swelled into a roar.

Then I saw the stream—a torrent of clear, tumbling water that raced along a rocky bed and broadened into a series of cascades over shallow rock ledges. Turning, I looked upstream and saw a crumbling dam about ten feet high, over which a foaming mass of white water plunged into a pool. Spray from the waterfall mingled with the rain.

The realtor was saying something about an old sawmill that had burned down.

Her words registered, but dimly.

She was pointing to a pile of stones that had been part of a foundation.

Details. Mere details. There would be time for them later. Right now I was too busy. I was falling in love.

That night it was impossible to sleep. As I lay in bed the words of the old saying came back to me: "Be careful what you ask for; you might get it." When I closed my eyes I saw the stream. The roar of the waterfall echoed in my ears.

I had to have it.

Never mind that Vermont was an eleven-hour drive from our Maryland home, where three of our children and my elderly mother also lived. Never mind that my psychotherapy practice was located there, a practice that had taken me years to build up, and my physicist husband was a professor at the University of Maryland. Never mind that I'd always been a saver, not a spender.

Details, mere details. All that mattered was the stream. It seemed to promise everything I longed for: freedom, oneness with nature, respite from a life in which I'd spent too much time taking care of people who were sick in body or mind. A chance to live in a place that made my heart rejoice, where I could grow into a different person. Not totally different—I wouldn't want that—but enough to renew a life that, at fifty, had grown stale and repetitive. I'd always wanted to write, but for years I'd let old habits get in the way and the needs of others come first.

I could write here. I was sure of it. I'd stumbled upon a place where I could become the person I was meant to be—and I hadn't even known that I was looking.

I'd never thought of myself as a spiritual person. I saw myself as somebody who adjusts. Practical, my mother would have said. Pragmatic. So it was hard to understand why, for the last three or four years, I'd had a feeling that Vermont was destined to become part of my life. I knew almost nothing about the state. I'd spent two days there when I was in my twenties, on a tour through New

England; that was all. Yet the idea stayed with me and kept growing stronger. It was hardly even an idea, more a word that hung in my mind like a hovering bird: Vermont, from the French words for "green" and "mountain."

Green mountain. It sounded restful, peaceful, cool. With a mysterious persistence, it drew me.

Recently I'd gotten in touch with an old friend I hadn't seen in thirty-five years. When she'd mentioned that she lived in Vermont, I'd thought, "Of course!" as if I already knew, though the last time I'd seen her she'd been living in New York. Now I'd just spent the weekend visiting her. Tomorrow I planned to go home. What I hadn't planned—or had I?—was that I would see a stream and suddenly my life would change. Could change, rather—whether or not it did was up to me. Fate had tossed me a challenge, a dare. The idea excited me.

I knew I could buy the property. By suburban standards it was very cheap. If I made an offer—and that was what you were supposed to do, only a fool would just flat-out say, "I'll take it"—I might get it for even less. But the realtor had said another buyer was interested. I wouldn't want to get into a bidding war . . .

I lay there wondering what to do and wishing I could fall asleep. If I were down the road in that old blue farmhouse right now, I could open the window and hear the sound of the water plunging over the dam, seeking its level, coursing toward an unknown sea.

I thought of a woman I hadn't seen in years. She lived in a wonderful house in a ravine with a stream at the bottom, a house that fitted her so well it almost seemed to define her. Although often rash and foolish, she could sometimes be wise. Years before she'd bought the wonderful house, she'd dickered for another house, one she really wanted. She'd lost it, and regretted it for a very long time. Finally she'd spotted her present house, and snapped it up at the asking price.

"When you fall in love with a house," she told me once, "don't bargain. Just buy it. You won't be sorry."

I was in love with a stream, but the principle seemed the same. Yes, I decided. I would buy the stream, and the blue house and ten acres that came with it.

I called my husband early the next morning and told him I'd seen a house I wanted to buy. We could spend the summers there, I said. He raised objections, but I stood my ground and to my surprise he agreed fairly quickly. He must have heard something different in my voice. That afternoon I wrote out a check for a deposit and gave it to the realtor.

Our first summer in Vermont I whipped the house into shape. I enjoyed going to flea markets and barn sales and picking up odds and ends of old country furniture, but I was impatient to start writing, for I felt I should. Hadn't I really bought the place to write, and didn't I have to prove that my impulsive purchase had been sensible? Actually, the answer to both questions was "No." The decision hadn't been sensible, not at all. It had come from the heart, not the head. And I didn't need to prove anything to my husband, for he had quickly settled into place at his computer and seemed content. But I was an impatient person who needed to see results right away. I was always trying to prove something, to others and to myself. I felt

under pressure to come up with answers, sometimes before I'd taken sufficient time to ponder the questions.

And I had guilt to exorcise. I'd left my children behind, and my aged mother. What kind of a mother, what
kind of a daughter did that make me? Even if it was only
for part of the summer, and my children were grown,
and my mother was doing well on her own. I'd put my
own needs first, which for a woman of my generation is
not easy; this was another reason I needed to prove I'd
been right.

But when I sat down at my brand-new computer the
words didn't come, even when I tried to force them. So
after a while I would leave the house and wander down
to the stream.

The first time I'd seen it I'd barely noticed how
choked the banks were with willow and birch saplings,
brambles and Tartarian honeysuckle. You could hardly
see the water. I started taking pruning shears with me
and made a few amateurish stabs at clearing away the
tangle of vegetation. Writing might be frustrating and
difficult, but the stream bank would be easier to con-
quer—or so I thought.

It proved to be harder than I'd expected. Although I
trimmed and snipped and clipped, I made only minor
inroads. In fact, before long the task began to seem overwhelming.

This was my first close encounter with the fecundity of
nature, which is at its most extreme where there is water,
especially foaming, splashing water that fills the air with
spray and encourages three new plants to spring up in the
place of every one you pull out or cut down. I had no idea
I was taking my first steps on the road to becoming a gar-

dener with one of the most difficult kinds of gardening imaginable. As I pored over a newly-purchased book by Gertrude Jekyll and studied the pictures of stream gardens in magazines, my fever mounted. There were no cautionary notes, no warnings to the unwary: "Proceed at Your Own Risk." Everything was made to seem easy.

The magazine version of gardening bears the same relation to real gardening by real people as the Hollywood version of romance does to the average person's love life. It took quite a while for me to realize this. The physical demands of stream gardening made it no easy task for a middle-aged, overweight, sedentary woman with a touch of arthritis in the knees. Those photographs in brilliant Ektachrome gave no hint of the slimy stones, the clambering up and down muddy, slippery banks, and the tumbles into the water that I actually experienced. The topic of mosquitoes, blackflies, deerflies, and mud wasps never came up in the gardening books I consulted. Beavers? The havoc they could wreak was passed over in silence. Nor was there a word about floods of snowmelt that could wash away flimsily-built structures and cover hopeful plantings with silt. There was certainly no mention of the money you should be prepared to spend, or the helpers you would have to hire, if you were serious about the enterprise.

Maybe a stream can be tamed single-handedly if you happen to be young, strong, totally committed to the project, and skilled in carpentry and stonemasonry as well as gardening. A cooperative spouse or partner would certainly help, though even then it wouldn't be easy.

Slapping away at the deerflies, whose bites were painful and swelled into hot, hard, aching lumps, I hacked at the undergrowth. I should have paid more attention to the stubs of old saplings I kept finding. Others had been here before me, yet the place looked as wild as if it had never been touched.

Ambitious plans raced through my mind for an arched Japanese bridge and a flight of steps down to the spongy little island from which the view of the falls was best; and of course there would be glorious plantings on the island and along the banks (which would first have to be cleared, a minor matter); and why not a gazebo, or a writing cabin?

I had become infected with my first bout of garden fever, a recurrent disease, like malaria: an obsessive state in which plan piles upon plan, project upon project, the more grandiose the better, and nothing, absolutely nothing, seems impossible.

I made a few inroads, but slowly, very slowly. I cleared my way around a large, mossy stone that reared up on the bank—a morning's work—and then wondered what to do with the brush I'd just strewn on the ground. The gardening books offered no clue, except for paeans to compost bins. These didn't seem to apply, since I was standing in the midst of a tiny space hemmed in by saplings that sprang up every few feet.

I tried throwing the cut branches over the bank into the stream, but this was not the solution. The branches weren't swept away by the current to some misty never-never land. They snagged on rocks and got stuck. They piled up. They looked bad.

Inspiration struck: I needed a "brush pile." It was a term I'd heard before but never taken to heart. How would I make one? And where would I put it? Out of sight, obviously, that was the point; in other words, some distance away. But how was I to get the stuff there? First I'd need to cut a path, no small task in itself since it would have to be wide enough to allow hefty branches to be dragged through it. And what about all the brush I'd have to cut down to make the path—where was that supposed to go?

I thought of asking my husband for help, but after thirty years of marriage there are certain things you know. Joe comes from a long line of scholars, and the belief that man's work (at least his) should be done indoors with his head, not outside with his hands, has become imprinted on his DNA. If I dragged him out here we would have a debate of Talmudic proportions over each twig, to determine whether and why it was truly necessary to cut it. Any broad principles we might establish would fail to carry over to the next twig, and the whole problem would have to be considered afresh. Every bite by a blackfly would cause lamentations that the wind would carry into the next county, and our neighbors would never take us seriously again.

There are battles I'd rather not engage in. Sighing, I stood before the boulder I had cleared, contemplating the patterns on its smooth, granite flanks. Lichens had sketched an irregular lacework of vaguely circular forms in gray, black, and gold; behind them I sensed a logic I couldn't begin to decipher.

I'd barely started the job of clearing the bank, and already I was tired. It's not that I was "out of condition"—this was my condition and had been for decades.

There was no place to sit except on the stone, but I didn't want to disturb the lichens' artwork. So I just folded my arms and stood there, discouraged. I no longer saw the stream, only the task I'd set for myself.

The water was still rushing. It never gave up, racing along in its rocky bed with a noise that was loud and insistent and indescribable. I stepped closer to the edge of the bank and peered through the leaves. In the bright sunlight the water splashed and flashed as it danced downstream like the essence of joy.

I watched it. My body relaxed. The sweet country air filled my lungs. I gazed, and thought of nothing.

A quarter of a mile down the road lived our nearest neighbor, an elderly widow named Blanche. Every time I drove to the general store I passed her little white house, perched on a rise near the stream. I noticed that the bank had been neatly cleared to expose the water. Not long after I met Blanche I asked her how she had managed this feat.

"Pruning shears," she said.

"That's all?" I'd hoped for a special technique I could learn, some canny Vermont folkway unknown to flatlanders like myself. I knew about pruning shears already, and the little handsaw I was using to cut down saplings. But as I would learn in time, most of gardening, like most of life, is fairly obvious. The main trick is keeping at it.

"Yep," she said. "And the lawnmower. 'Course if you want to spend money you could get a man to brush-hog it."

I didn't know what brush-hogging was, but it sounded drastic, like a buzz haircut. I didn't want to get involved with something I couldn't control, something that might wipe out, for example, the jack-in-the-pulpit

I'd found growing on the bank. "Your stream looks nice," I said a bit wistfully.

"I don't do much." Her mouth gave the sour little downturn I would come to know.

"I think it looks lovely."

She shook her head as we surveyed the stream. "Used to look a lot better. I used to keep at it, but it was no use. Too much work, just have to keep doing it over again. Like housework, really." Blanche knew a lot about housework, as she was employed as a housekeeper by a family down the road. "I used to keep ducks down there." She gave the satisfied nod of a pessimist whose dim view of life has been confirmed. "Fox got every last one of them."

"I love the way the water forms a little pool."

She sniffed. "Beavers love it, too. Last month they dammed up the culvert. Every morning I took the sticks away, and every night they put them back. Can't win that game! Finally had to call the game warden."

"And what happened?"

"Shot 'em. I told him, 'You didn't have to do that.' Thought maybe he'd take them someplace else in one of those Hav-a-Heart traps, but he told me, 'I'm not running no taxi service for no beavers.' Mother was real upset when she heard." Blanche's ninety-three-year-old mother lived across the road in the small house painted barn red in which Blanche had been born. In the old days, before the sawmill had burned down, Blanche's mother had cooked for the owner and the workers in the house that now belonged to me. The owner hadn't believed in daylight saving time. "He kept to the old time," Blanche told me. "He said it was better. Finally my mother had to quit. It threw her whole day off."

Reassured by my conversation with Blanche that I wasn't doing anything really wrong, I continued clearing around the waterfall. Every day brought discoveries—a raspberry thicket, a patch of tiny wild orchids, a long piece of tubing wedged in the stream (evidently water had been drawn out in the past for some inscrutable purpose), scattered bricks and rough columns of cut stone from the old sawmill that had once stood there.

I clipped and sawed and dragged and piled. I crossed and re-crossed the stream on a slippery timber that someone had wedged between the stones. I pondered thirty-foot pines atop old stone walls and wondered how long it had taken them to grow to their present height. Occasionally I was startled by a trout, looking impossibly large in the shallow water. I brushed pine needles from a long, flat-topped rock that was just the right height for a bench, and sat there writing in a notebook I'd started leaving beside the stream in a plastic bag.

Gradually I spent more time writing in my notebook and less time clearing brush. I jotted down random thoughts, scraps of poetry, and memories of the childhood summers I'd spent playing in the brook behind my grandparents' house in the Catskills. Somehow the stream made writing easier. It seemed to wash away my need to prove things. I simply wrote. When I reached the last page of the notebook it felt natural to make the transition to the computer in the room I'd fixed up as a study but hardly ever used.

I'd brought a chair down to the stream—the rock on which I'd sat at first was too cold except when the sun shone directly on it—but I seldom used it now. I found myself visiting the stream less often. After all, it was across the road and a fair distance from the house. When I went outdoors I could hear the sound, though, a comforting background noise that was present whether or not I paid any attention to it.

By the end of the summer, shoots had begun to appear at the base of some of the saplings I'd cut down. I could have trimmed them away—I did trim a few—but of course there were all the other saplings I hadn't gotten around to at all yet, and perhaps I should tackle those first. Only I'd forgotten to bring the saw—or the clippers.

I still loved the stream, but not in the same way. It seemed to be making demands on me. Provoking a certain guilt. At least the work I'd done had made it possible to see the waterfall more clearly. I could climb down the bank on some wobbly stones I'd set in place for steps.

But the unsightly brush pile loomed in plain view (tucking it out of sight had seemed like too much work), and the little island where I'd wanted to place a picnic table proved to be squishy underfoot and inhabited by mud wasps. Solutions could have been found to these problems, but I never got around to looking for them seriously. I was too busy writing.

How I Became
a Gardener

Sweet Cicely is a great pretender. A perennial herb that grows as large as a shrub, it has fern-like foliage, flowers that resemble Queen Anne's Lace, and a flavor like licorice.

A fine, shapely Sweet Cicely flourishes against the south wall of my house in splendid isolation, quarantined from the rest of the garden by a wide swath of lawn that has managed to contain her wandering ways for years now. Even so, I keep a wary eye on her and root out any seedlings she may drop, because I know a garden not a mile from here where the hussy has flung herself indiscriminately into every bed and then slunk into the shrub border, where she lurks in the shadows like a dangerous beast. Still, Sweet Cicely is one of my favorite plants, not just for her good looks but because she reminds me of Adele Dawson, who gave me the original seedling.

I heard Adele's name soon after I came to Vermont. This was the weekend when I first saw the old blue farm- house and the stream. I'd driven up to spend some time with my childhood friend, Anita. Just a visit, I'd thought. But as the road wound between the Green Mountains a sense of peace came over me such as I hadn't felt in years, and I wondered if I could find a way to spend more time here, perhaps even buy a summer house.

Anita and the couple she'd invited over to meet me encouraged this notion, so I began to elaborate on it. "I've always wanted to live near water," I said, and knew when I heard the words that they were true. "Not the ocean. A stream—maybe even a waterfall."

They looked at each other, and Anita's friend Mary said, "She wants a house like Adele's."

"Who's Adele?"

"An eighty-year-old woman"—Adele's exact age, I would learn, was usually remarked on in any mention of her—"who lives in a wonderful old house next to the longest waterfall in the state of Vermont."

I said, "Maybe she'd sell it."

"Oh, no."

I'm ashamed to admit that I said next, "Maybe she'll die." I'd come of age in New York during the postwar housing shortage, which made people ruthless. "Or go into a nursing home."

There was a gasp. I knew I'd said the wrong thing. Vermont was not New York.

Anita tried to smooth things over. "You don't know her. She's a remarkable woman."

"A writer, an artist." Mary put in.

"An herbalist—she's written a book about herbs. Her garden is amazing. Some people say she's a witch. She'll probably live forever."

"And she's a very sensuous woman," Mary's husband, Bob, added rather solemnly.

Adele had been married three times, they told me. Or was it four? Had five children living in other states—or was it six?—and many grandchildren. An elderly gentleman was courting her, but she'd refused to marry him, said he was too old for her. My friend said, "Adele told me once, 'I don't know what's wrong with men. They always want to marry me.'"

She'd come to Vermont with the last of her husbands when she was sixty-four. One winter had been enough for him, and he'd told her he was moving down to Florida. She'd said, "You should. It sounds just right for you. I'm staying here." At sixty-five she'd reinvented herself and become a person her children didn't recognize. That was when she'd started growing herbs and taking in a succession of young men, most of them more or less down on their luck. In exchange for help with the chores, she provided a home, companionship, travel, a share in her social life—which grew more rich and varied every year—and excellent cooking. Nobody knew for sure if the arrangement ended there, but people wondered.

Change isn't easy. Sometimes I wonder if it is even possible. As a psychotherapist I've watched many people make the effort to transform themselves, and I've tried to help with the process. Maybe the new self was there all along, like a hidden spring, and all I've done is assist in clearing away the debris so the waters can flow into the light of day. Many times I've struggled to change myself. Certain people seem to think that real change occurs only when someone becomes completely different in some basic way—heterosexual instead of homosexual, thin instead of fat. Yet I believe it is just as important to learn to accept unwelcome truths about oneself and incorporate them creatively into one's life, often by living in a different way.

I don't really believe in epiphanies, although short story editors relish them. Change usually comes about as the result of a long, gradual, largely internal process that may be invisible until a dramatic gesture reveals it to the world—like Adele's remaining in Vermont after her husband had departed.

Pretending is part of the process. For a while one has to act as if one were a certain kind of person, trying on a new role to see if it can be made to fit.

Adele must have been a great and brave pretender, judging from the person she had become by the time I met her. This meeting took place two years after I had first heard of her. My husband and I were still settling into the old farmhouse we'd bought. The land around the house was overgrown with weeds and brush, and I hadn't even thought about trying to make a garden.

One day I stopped at the two-room country library I'd been meaning for some time to explore. Inside, at a table facing the door, sat a diminutive, freckled old person of indeterminate gender wearing a T-shirt and jeans, with white hair cut short like a boy's, and a very straight back. She was arranging index cards in a box with brisk efficiency. Since she was the only one there, I assumed she was the librarian and asked if I could take out a li-

brary card. She explained that she was only a volunteer.
"But maybe I could figure out how to do it," she said
with a playful, self-deprecating laugh. Her teeth were
yellow and twisted, almost fang-like; they made her look
like a witch. "It can't be that hard."

When I told her my name she acted very impressed.
She'd just been reading a mystery story I'd written and
told me enthusiastically that she'd loved it. She intro-
duced herself and I realized that this was the famous
Adele. "Come and visit me!" she urged. "Come any time!
Do you know where I live?" I said I did—she didn't seem
surprised—and she repeated, "Come any time at all!
Only don't come tomorrow because I'm driving to
California."

"Really? Alone?"

"No, I'm taking two dogs. But I'll be back in a
month."

I left the library trying to make the picture of Adele
I'd formed in my mind merge with the person I'd just
met. The real Adele hadn't seemed larger than life. I
didn't think an aged herbalist should be bubbly.
Sensuous? Forget it. And those teeth!

Still, how many women of eighty-two would be up to
driving cross-country, with or without dogs? At least her
fabled vigor hadn't been exaggerated.

Curious to see her house and the waterfall as well as
her garden, of which I had heard much, I resolved to
visit her.

But Labor Day came, my husband returned to
Maryland to resume teaching, a cousin arrived to see the
foliage and help me close up the house, and I still hadn't
visited Adele.

She was on my mind, though.

Early one morning my cousin and I loaded our bags in the car and set out on the long journey home. We drove a mile or two in silence, and then she said, "So what's the matter?"

"There's one thing I didn't do."

"What?"

"Somebody I meant to visit."

I told her about Adele, and she suggested we stop at her house, which was not far out of our way. We drove a few miles further and turned onto a steep dirt road, roaring uphill until we reached a little white clapboard house hugging a rise. The steep bank between the house and the road was thick with daylilies and old roses, ferns and Siberian irises. Through the tangle, fireweed and the tall silver plumes of artemisia ran wild. Earlier in the season someone had pointed out to me the purple flowers of the fireweed and said that Adele had transplanted them from the wild, something she often did, with notable success. Now they had gone to seed and were filling the air with a fine, white fluff that settled on our shoulders and hair as we climbed the wooden steps to the porch.

A sagging wicker armchair faced west, and a trowel had been left on the well-worn cushion. Overhead fluttered the blue-and-white banner covered with oriental calligraphy of which I'd already been told, brought by a friend from Japan. One day a Japanese family had appeared at her door, and assuming they'd come to see the garden she'd showed them around. She'd served them tea in her teahouse. It was very pleasant, but as time passed and the family lingered, she'd finally said, "I have to work in the garden now."

"But where is the ice?" the man had asked.

The handsome calligraphy on the banner meant "Ice for Sale."

A hand-painted sign hung on the door, welcoming the visitor with a paean to the garden, and to the sun, and to the Great Spirit and so forth. It seemed to me a bit much.

Some distance away lay another sign that said, "Not at home! Scram! Go away! This means you!" I'd heard she sometimes hung it on the door on hot days. When her friends stopped by, though, they would decide the sign didn't apply to them and walk through the house and out the back door, occasionally finding her at work in the garden in the nude, having discarded her clothes, piece by piece, to cool off. Then she would scramble around the hill trying to find them and putting them on, meanwhile talking and smiling hospitably.

When I knocked there was no answer. The door stood ajar, so we stepped inside and found ourselves in the kitchen. My cousin, who is an interior decorator in New York, looked around and said, "Oh my God, this is incredible."

The room was dark and smelled wonderful. Bunches of herbs hung, drying, from nails hammered into the smoke-darkened beams. On the stove in a cast-iron cauldron something rich and aromatic simmered. Warmth radiated from a potbellied woodstove next to which a big copper tub held logs and kindling. All the appliances were old-fashioned, the wooden table and chairs looked a bit shaky, and the counters and windowsills were crowded with vessels for cooking and food storage, as well as stoppered jars of salves and tinctures with "Adele's No. 2—for sprains" and the like hand-written on the labels. Although crowded, the kitchen was well organized and rather neat. More signs were tacked up on the walls. One, which now hangs in my own kitchen, read: "People who read their poetry out loud may have other unpleasant habits."

"You think it's all right to just walk in?" my cousin said.

"I don't know." I was heading for the back door, and she followed me out into a blaze of early morning light. Everywhere, dewdrops sparkled like prisms. We could hear the rushing of the waterfall but couldn't see it. Just beyond a narrow lawn with a picnic table on it, Adele's garden climbed a steep slope. It had no regularity of plan but seemed to have evolved spontaneously from the energies of its creator. It was a big, exuberant, shaggy garden, the kind that is hospitable to happy accidents, accommodating plants once common but now so old-fashioned they had become rare; a garden where plants were used in unconventional ways, like the flowering raspberry trained over the kitchen door that Adele later told us she'd brought in from the wild.

Halfway up the hill we saw her on her knees, weeding. She stood up, waving both arms in greeting, and darted nimbly down a steep path crying, "Hello! Hello! I've been wondering when you would come to see me! You can help me weed! And this is?" I introduced my cousin and said we were heading south for the winter. "And you decided to drop in before you left! What a good idea! Come inside, or would you like to see the garden first?"

"We can't stay long."

"Oh, there's time for a cup of tea. We can have it in the teahouse." She pointed uphill where, high above us, the roof of a small wooden structure peeped through the leaves. "A young man who used to live here built it for me as a gift. It's completely authentic, he spent three years in Japan studying Zen. You know, I once married a couple in the teahouse, well not married, exactly, but they thought it was just as good." She laughed. "And I'm sure it was! They're still together!"

My cousin was wearing high heels, so we settled for a quick tour of the borders beside the lawn. They were crowded with healthy-looking plants, which Adele named for us, handing us leaves to rub between our fingers and put to our noses. Some smelled sweet while others were spicy or medicinal.

"Feel this," she said. She stooped to nip a couple of silvery leaves, passed them lightly across her cheek and handed them to us. I stroked the one I'd been given. The texture was velvety, sensual. "Lamb's Ear. I'll give you a piece some time. Here, try this." She plucked a seed-pod from a plant covered with large pink flowers—a mallow, although I didn't then know its name. "Try it?"

Her agile fingers spread the pod, revealing a neat button of seeds. She popped a few into her mouth to encourage us. Cautiously, I nibbled one. "Good," I said, and ate the rest.

"Country people call it 'cheese' because it's round, like a cheese. The leaves are good for mosquito bites. Or you can use them in salad." We moved on. "This one is Lady's Mantle—Alchemilla. It's a blood coagulant." She pointed out the glistening drop of dew cradled in each rounded leaf and said the alchemists used to gather these drops for their magic potions. On the same spot some years later I would meet an Albanian seeress with blazing eyes who had come to visit with her entourage, including a photographer whose mission was to photograph at dawn a dewdrop on Adele's Lady's Mantle.

We came to a massive plant at the end of a bed. Adele said, "Try these," and snapped off a handful of narrow seeds, each one the length of my little fingernail.

I nibbled. The seeds tasted of anise. "These are delicious! I love licorice—I always pick out the black jellybeans. What is this plant?"

My enthusiasm seemed to delight her. She smiled, showing her fang-like yellow teeth, and I wondered if she really was a witch. Not that I believed in witches, but in her presence my beliefs seemed to float off into irrelevance. Certainly she seemed to have found the secret of eternal youth. I wasn't at all afraid of her; if she was a witch she must be a good one. Adele said, "It's called Sweet Cicely. I'll give you a piece some time." Nearby, a trowel had been left thrust into the earth. She noticed it and said, "Oh, I'll give you a piece right now." She dug up a seedling that was growing beside the mother plant and, as long as she was bending over anyway, pulled a few weeds and tossed them into a tidy pile. She stood up and tipped the trowel carefully into my hand. "Here. For your garden."

"But I don't have a garden."

Looking into my eyes she said firmly, "You will."

Was it a prediction or a command? I didn't know, but a spark of something had passed between us. The warm rootball nestled into my palm like a baby bird, and the little plant looked perky. Adele gave it the lightest of pats, a casual benediction, and pronounced, "It will grow. Just water it."

For the moment I quite forgot that I was on my way home for the winter. Behind Adele's back my cousin raised her eyebrows at me as, helplessly, we trailed our hostess into the house. She showed me how to transfer the seedling to an empty yogurt cup. Then I accepted the first of the many cups of tea I was to drink in her kitchen over the years.

When my cousin and I finally got into the car, we sat for a while looking at the seedling clutched in my hand. Then she started the motor. "We have to go back," she said.

"I know."

Neither of us mentioned the ten-hour trip. What was the point?

We drove back to my house. I unlocked it and went up to the loft, where I thought I'd seen an old shovel. Yes, it was there. I carried it outside. With the yogurt cup in one hand and the shovel in the other, I clambered around the hummocks in the yard until I came to a level place on the sunny side of the house. Clumsily, I scraped away the weeds and tried pushing the point of the shovel into the dirt, which was surprisingly soft and rich, not hard as I'd expected. I bore down with my foot on the shovel, which slipped into the earth as if it knew the way, and dug a nice, roomy hole. I planted the seedling. Then, since the house water was turned off, I filled a pail at the stream and poured water carefully around the plant. It still looked perky.

And so I became a gardener.

The Boundary Pine

As we settled into the blue farmhouse I gradually became more aware of the forest behind the clearing. It covered a west-facing hill and consisted of twenty acres of stately white pines that enjoyed a certain local fame because they were the tallest in the vicinity.

These woods did not belong to us. They were the property of a wealthy neighbor who had retired to Vermont and invested in timberland. I'd barely noticed them when we'd bought the house, for to me, woods were woods. My life had been spent in cities and suburbs, and woods were alien places. I'd had little experience of them and I gave them no thought. Certainly I didn't consider them as living organisms that might have puzzling histories and uncertain futures—creatures not totally unlike myself—or think that biographies full of incident could be written about them, marked by good years and bad and above all by change, whether slow and imperceptible or sudden and violent.

A couple of months went by before I even set foot in the woods. They attracted me, but I was afraid of them. It was a visceral fear I didn't care to acknowledge or examine. After all, what was there to be afraid of? Tigers and boa constrictors didn't lurk in the Vermont woods. Still, as I explored the clearing around our house—a "clearing" only in comparison to the surrounding forest, for it was overgrown with weedy trees and brush—I kept my distance from the wall of towering pines.

My fear of the woods made me feel foolish; it seemed a flaw in my character. Yet my feelings were hardly unique, even if my Vermont neighbors did not share them and would have laughed at me if they had known about them. My neighbors hunted deer and other animals during hunting season, culled trees for lumber and firewood, and gathered maple syrup in the spring. Still, woods are trackless, confusing places to those who don't know how to read their signs and landmarks, and it is quite possible to lose your way in them. As a child I'd read stories of people who wandered in the woods for hours and days, circling back on their tracks without realizing it. Even primitive peoples who rely on the woods for their livelihood preserve a sense of awe about them, believing that spirits or the souls of the dead dwell in the trees, and that these can be menacing.

Our house had come with "spring rights" to our wealthy neighbor's land, a concept new to me that meant we had the right to draw water from a certain spring in his woods, halfway up the hill. This was the water we drank every day, for an underground pipe led from the spring to the house. One day it occurred to me that we should test the water. We should climb the hill, take a look at the spring, and draw a sample.

My husband, who is happiest indoors, pointed out that we could just as well take a sample from the faucet in the kitchen. But I insisted. The woods had begun to interest me. Morning after morning when my husband was still asleep I would watch the sun rise over the lofty pines, until the shapes of individual trees had become familiar to me, like the faces of neighbors I saw at the general store. I wanted to get to know the woods better, but I wasn't going in there alone.

Joe allowed himself to be dragged along. Even with him beside me I felt nervous as we ducked through the low-hanging branches that curtained the edge of the woods. Our kitchen door was still in sight, but technically we were trespassing. What if the owner suddenly appeared?

We began to climb the hill, my husband complaining at the lumpiness of the ground, the scratchiness of the underbrush, and the aggressiveness of the mosquitoes. I didn't find it easy going either. If there was a knack to walking in woods like these, it was one I'd never acquired. The earth was strewn with fallen trees, some with sharp, entangling branches that snatched at my ankles and others with rotten trunks that gave way unexpectedly under my feet. The ground seemed to consist entirely of humps and hollows, up and down which I floundered, waving my arms to keep my balance. Trees had been falling and rotting away here for generations, it seemed, creating these ripples in the surface of the earth. I'd always taken for granted a certain flatness underfoot, having spent my life in places where bulldozers I'd never needed to think about had gone before me, smoothing my way. I had expected the woods to look something like a park (I knew parks), but they didn't—not at all. They seemed littered and primitive, an exotic environment where you could fall and break a bone; a place of secret rustlings where, when you turned your head, you saw nothing.

We hunted around for a while. Any local child would have known enough to follow the gully that, having been dug out by the overflow of the spring, naturally led straight to it. But this didn't occur to us. Eventually, my eye was caught by a straight, horizontal line that proved to be the edge of a large wooden box half-buried in the ground. We worked our way over more hummocks until we reached it. The box had a sloping lid covered by a sheet of galvanized metal that was almost hidden by a thick layer of pine needles. We brushed them aside and cautiously raised the lid.

Inside the box lay a rectangle of perfectly still, clear water about two feet deep. We leaned forward to look down into it and saw the reflection of our faces. Behind our heads, a few bright glimpses of sky pierced the darkness of the forest canopy. Wordlessly, we looked at each other. There seemed something magical about this hidden pool, which had lain for years waiting for us to find it.

Could it be this simple? You sank a box with an open bottom into the ground in the right place and inserted a pipe. You dug a trench down the hill and buried the pipe in it. The pipe carried the water to your house.

For the first time, I really grasped where water came from. You didn't necessarily need distant reservoirs, aqueducts that were marvels of engineering, or tons of chlorine and other chemicals. You didn't need pumps that stopped working during power failures, or water meters and the men who came to read them with cans of Mace on their belts to fend off dogs. You didn't even need monthly bills. All you had to have was a good spring and the force of gravity.

The water, when we had it tested, turned out to be perfectly pure. It was also delicious, especially compared to the chlorine-flavored water that flowed from our faucets in Maryland.

Fall came before I entered the woods again. My husband returned to Maryland to teach, but after some hesitation I decided to remain in Vermont a while longer and watch the leaves turn. I'd never stayed alone before in a place from which I couldn't see another house, and the idea made me uneasy; it also challenged me, like a test I had to pass.

I drove Joe to the airport and saw him off. On the way back I stopped to browse in a bookstore in Montpelier. A book caught my eye, a volume of short stories by Janet Kauffman called *Places in the World a Woman Could Walk*. The title had a powerful resonance for me. I'd come to feel that there weren't many such places, and over the years they seemed to have become scarcer.

In the Washington area where I'd lived for so long, I took more and more precautions. This had become a habit, but so gradually that I hadn't realized how much of my life had come to be controlled by fear. I was always hearing stories on TV and in the papers and from friends. So I locked my doors. In parking lots I made sure to look in my car before getting inside—a co-worker of mine had been raped and beaten by a man hiding in the back seat. Taking a shortcut through an alley or a stretch of woods was out of the question. These were places where bad things happened to women, and everyone knew it—all you had to do was read those helpful tips by the police that told women how to survive, as if we were an endangered species.

Yet each time I took the long way around—just to be safe, just to live a little longer—anger would well up in me and poison my day.

All these evasions had become a part of me. Though necessary, they narrowed me as a person and as a writer. I wondered if Vermont might be a place in the world where I could walk with more freedom than I'd enjoyed in a long time.

A woman who lived on our dirt road had told me she never locked her door. "One of my neighbors might need something when I'm out," she'd said, as if it were the most natural thing in the world.

Another neighbor, a widow in her seventies, happened to mention taking a shortcut through the woods.

"Aren't you scared?" I said.

"Of what?"

I looked at her. "Oh—you know," I said. I felt I didn't know her well enough to use the word "rape," yet that was what we were talking about, wasn't it? It was rape the police were warning us about, rape that kept women from walking wherever they wanted to go. I said, "Oh, getting lost."

She looked right back at me. "Used to spend the whole day in the woods when I was younger, hunting. Never got lost as far as I know. If you head downhill you're bound to come to a road—around here, anyway. Don't know how it is someplace else."

It was midafternoon when I got back from the airport. The old blue house was still but not quiet. The refrigerator hummed, turning itself on and off. Birds were singing. Insects still chirred, though it was late in the season. I could hear the rushing of the stream across the road. I was alone, and it felt good. I sat outside and read *Places in the World a Woman Could Walk,* slapping at the occasional deerfly. Now and then I eyed the woods, taking their measure.

The next day it rained and I stayed indoors. I thought about the fact that Vermont had the lowest crime rate in the nation, that people still didn't lock their doors or their cars, and that shopkeepers took your check without asking to see your driver's license.

On the third day the sun shone. After I washed my breakfast dishes I set out across the clearing. The distance from the house to the edge of the woods wasn't great, but the unevenness of the ground slowed me down. I skirted an old dump filled with broken bottles and rusty pots and pans, and slogged my way through the swampy area where I sank up to my ankles in the muck.

Then the ground tilted upward and the soil became firmer. I walked up to the boundary tree, a lofty pine into which a metal marker with the name of the owner's timber company had been hammered, six feet above the ground. Beyond the pine the woods beckoned, dim and cool.

I laid my hand on the trunk, which felt as solid as a house, and edged forward through the curtain of pine branches. My hand still touching the boundary tree, I leaned forward like a swimmer about to dive into the water. I looked around. A thick layer of pine needles covered the ground. Here and there were boulders the size of baby elephants, their silver-gray backs blotched with lichens.

My hand remained glued to the tree trunk. Far overhead, narrow shafts of light pierced the forest canopy. It was very quiet, as if my appearance had interrupted something, silenced whatever had been going on a moment earlier. Then a squirrel chattered and ran across a branch, flicking its tail. Slowly, my hand detached itself from the tree. I stepped over to a fern that was growing about ten feet away. I leaned down and inspected it, my heart pounding. Some distance away I saw another fern. It seemed to be a different kind. "Tomorrow I'll buy a fern book," I thought.

Straightening, I took a deep breath.

Then I went for a walk in the woods.

My first.

Lady's-Slippers

Few plants have more mystique than the showy lady's-slipper, also sometimes known as the pink lady's-slipper, the largest of the wild orchids native to the northeastern United States. It has the lure of the forbidden, for it is protected by law in many localities, and digging it up from the wild is strongly discouraged. In the swamps and woodlands where it once flourished it has become rare, and it is seldom encountered in gardens. The showy lady's-slipper demands intensely acid soil and is partial to extravagant quantities of pine needles. Its clumps are very fragile and difficult to divide successfully. "Use great care," warns Henry W. Art in his book on wildflowers. As for growing the showy lady's-slipper from seed, my copy of Taylor's *Encyclopedia of Gardening*, usually so helpful, notes only: "Satisfactory propagation method unknown at time of writing."

The only place I ever saw the showy lady's-slipper growing was in the garden of my neighbor, Blanche, and it
took a while before I noticed it. Blanche has spent her
entire life in Vermont. As a newcomer I often asked her
advice. When we first moved to Vermont she was in her
seventies and very fit. Her hair was still dark brown—
perhaps dyed, I wasn't sure—and stiffly coiffed, as if she
set it in pin curls before going to bed. I used to see her up
on the sloping roof with a long-handled push broom,
sweeping off the layer of needles that had fallen from the
big pine tree next to her house. Otherwise the needles
would rot the tarpaper, she told me. This chore she did
twice every fall, climbing up on an aluminum ladder she
kept in the garage. I once told her I'd be afraid to go up
there. She replied matter-of-factly, "I'm not afraid of
heights. I used to sweep snow off people's roofs and
paint houses."

Blanche's garden was small. Out front she had a rectangle of good dirt about the same size as her little
house, and a local farmer rototilled it for her every
spring. There Blanche would plant vegetables and a row
or two of flowers. I seldom saw her in the garden when I
drove past, but she obviously lavished much time on it.
Each bean plant had its neat tripod of cut saplings to
climb, and every tomato plant emerged out of the top of
a brown paper grocery bag with a couple of slits cut in
the bottom. Cucumbers were protected from cutworms
by plastic gallon jugs, and scraps of bright tinfoil fluttered on strings to frighten away the birds.

Despite all this tender care, Blanche never had a good word to say about her garden. She practiced "Evil Eye" gardening, reminding me of my Russian-born grandmother, who believed that praising the object of your affection calls up malign forces that might snatch it away. "Beans this year just plain amounted to nothing," Blanche would say. "Might as well plow the whole row under." Or, "I don't know why I trouble to plant tomatoes. Frost gets them before I do." She never had a good word for her flowers, either, and to hear her tell it she planned to tear them all out next week and never plant another.

Blanche's most scathing scorn was reserved for her tuberous begonias. These she grew in a window box running the length of her house that faced the road, and they just couldn't do anything right. It was a wonder she flaunted the miserable things so publicly, year after year. Each fall before the first frost she carefully cut off the tops and added them to her compost pile. Then she dug up the tubers and laid them on a bed of peat moss inside tin cookie boxes; the lids had air-holes punched by her late husband. All winter she stored them on a shelf in the cellar. I don't know what she added to the soil in the window boxes to freshen it, but it must have been potent stuff.

The following spring Blanche would bring all the tubers upstairs and start them growing in pots on the windowsills. "They're a nuisance," she would say. "They take such a long time. They use up all the room." Every year they grew more magnificent, at least to my eyes, with huge flowers shaped like roses and gardenias and carnations, in glowing tones of yellow, pink, and red. She took her pessimistic time planting them out in the window box, for she'd seen her share of late spring frosts and could describe the havoc each had wreaked, going back years.

But every spring a day would finally come when Blanche planted out the begonias, spacing them evenly in the long window box and leaving plenty of room for each one to spread. Although the plants would still be small, most already sported a few enormous blossoms. "Not worth a darn," she would say when I stopped to admire them. "Won't be as good as last summer, even, and that was terrible. Nothing but slugs and mildew. I put the bulbs down cellar and half of them died on me. I don't know what's wrong with them. Just sickly, I guess."

Over the years I came to have a better understanding of why Blanche disparaged her garden. I do the same thing, and so do other gardeners I know. This is because the gardener and the visitor see two different gardens. The visitor responds to the garden before her eyes—its colors, scents, mossy stones, pleasing curves, the shapes of the flowers, perhaps an inviting bench—and says quite sincerely, "How beautiful!" But the gardener sees the garden that exists in her own mind, where all the weeds have been pulled, the poppies thinned, the foxglove seedlings transplanted, the delphiniums staked, the saucer of beer set out to drown the slugs, the unhappy primula moved from that dry, sunny spot to a moist, shady one.

The gardener is always painfully aware of the gap between the dream and the reality. Like every artist, she knows that whatever is achieved is nevertheless a betrayal of that first radiant vision. So she keeps apologizing. When referring to the garden's shortcomings, she is really talking about her own. She knows she could have worked a little longer or a little harder, braved a few more blackflies, and watered the transplants instead of hoping for rain to save her the trouble. Gardening, like a religious discipline or any other truly worthwhile activity, daily brings us face to face with our own weaknesses, even as it holds out a hope for repentance and reform at some indefinite time in the future.

Like religion, too, gardening confronts us with the hard questions, such as why bad things happen to good people. Just when we have finally seeded the wildflower meadow-to-be and the seedlings are beginning to emerge, the arduous work of clearing and digging and raking and eliminating the weeds now complete, why does a record-breaking drought have to set in? Why, when we have coddled the delphiniums until they reach their absolute peak, must a violent windstorm come along and snap off their heads? Why does the white rugosa rose, purchased in good faith from a reputable nursery, prove as soon as it unfurls its first blossoms to be infested with hundreds of yellow and brown beetles that quickly spread to the rest of the garden? Why, why, why?

Blanche believed in staying busy. During the Fourth of July parade, when people from the surrounding region crowded the town, she dispensed cider and homemade doughnuts and presided over the historical exhibit in the old town hall. When fall came, she contributed a large pan of red-flannel hash to the Harvest Supper and coordinated the events that took place in the village during Foliage Days, a week-long celebration in which six towns got together to provide activities for visiting leaf peepers that brought a little extra money into the region.

In the weeks before the festivities Blanche kept an anxious eye on the hills. "Leaves aren't so good this year," she would say, although to me they looked spectacular. "Not enough red."

"Blanche, you say that every year."

"It was too dry this summer." Or too wet, or too cold, or too warm at a critical point. "They won't hold off. They'll peak before Foliage Days." She would shake her head. "Guess I can't do anything about it. Care for some pie? Apple—I baked it this morning, didn't turn out too good but if you want a piece you can have it."

I'd known Blanche and her garden for several years before I noticed her lady's-slippers. They weren't hidden, exactly, but they were tucked into a corner between the house and the garage, and I'd never happened to stop by when they were in bloom.

The first time I saw them I exclaimed, "What are those!" I thought I knew, but I could hardly believe it.

"Lady's-slippers," she said nonchalantly.

The clump was at least three feet across, and thick with stiff, oval leaves. Above them on narrow green stalks danced the puffy, orchidlike flower sacs. I said, "Where on earth did you find them?"

She smiled, a smile that lacked her usual tartness. "Down by the old dump, in a cow pasture. My father knew about them. He used to hunt and trap down there. Me too—I caught foxes and coons."

"What did you do with them?"

"Skun 'em. Sold the skins. And what was left, people would buy—the coons, anyway. They're good eating. Nobody'll eat a fox."

I asked her if she'd found the lady's-slippers hard to grow, and she nodded. "Had to make three tries before they would take. I don't know why, I just couldn't get them to hold over. I had to keep going back."

"They look fine now. What do you do for them?"

"Pine needles." She gestured toward the huge white pine that sheltered her house. It was what is called a "wolf tree," not narrow and straight like a forest pine but with massive side branches, typical of a tree that has grown up in isolation and received light from the sides as well as from above. The tree showered Blanche's yard with needles that had to be raked off the grass as well as swept off the roof. The needles made wonderful mulch.

We stood together gazing down at the lady's-slippers. The flowers were beautiful but strange, the upper petals narrow, twisted, and greenish-white, the engorged lower sacs shot with pink and red veining like blood vessels. Blanche said, "I give them pine needles every year." Her voice had grown tender, almost doting. "Twice—in the spring and the fall. They're the only thing I baby."

I got into the habit of dropping in on Blanche every summer when the lady's-slippers were in bloom. The flowers appeared in June and lasted only a few weeks; when they bloomed they were superb.

Lady's-slippers in the wild have been picked and dug until they are now extremely rare. They remain a tempting target, for although transplanting has its perils, it is really the only way to possess them. Raising lady's-slippers from seed is so difficult that for most gardeners it is simply impossible—and this includes nurserymen, who would dearly love to be able to offer them for sale in commercial quantities. At every stage in the process, obstacles present themselves. The first problem is obtaining enough seeds, for although the blossoms can produce 50,000 seeds, they must first be pollinated, and few insects are willing to cooperate. Although the engorged pink sacs with their deep central grooves look inviting, the orchids produce no nectar and most insects pass them by.

Once the seeds germinate, they remain hidden underground for several years, forming a symbiotic relationship with a certain primitive fungus that brings them nutrients until they are mature enough to grow root hairs. Unfortunately, this essential fungus also has a tendency to make the seeds rot. If a seed nevertheless survives long enough to send up a shoot, the plant will require just the right amount of sun, moisture, and acidity to thrive. Finally the first flower may appear—as much as fifteen years later.

Because of these problems, cloning has long been the Holy Grail of scientific efforts to propagate the lady's-slipper. Every few years rumors of a successfully cloned lady's-slipper sweep the plant world, only to fade away. Not long ago I read that a New Hampshire high school girl had managed to clone one for a science fair project. Maybe so, but I see no signs that the orchids are about to come on the market.

In all the times I visited Blanche's lady's-slippers, I never saw her frown at them or belittle them in any way. Once when we'd had a particularly rainy spring she remarked, looking down at them, "I think this is the best year they ever had."

I wondered why she was so different with her lady's-slippers. Was it just that they were rare, a trophy attesting to her skill as a gardener? Did they remind her of her long-dead father, or of Wilford, her late husband, who'd gone with her to dig them up? "Thirty-five years ago it was, before he got the emphysema," she told me once. "We carried them out in pails. They were real heavy, with all the dirt we took."

She had met Wilford at a Valentine's Day dance when she was still in high school, and they had gone together for four years before marrying, because she wasn't in any hurry to settle down. "He was from Canada and his parents never did learn English," she said. "So I couldn't fight with them too much. He made our furniture. Wilford liked to work, he always had work on his mind."

Maybe the lady's-slippers were the nearest thing in her life to perfection. Or maybe she had a reason about which she never even dropped a hint. If so, that's as it should be. Every garden should have some secrets, some hidden treasures.

In the last few years Blanche has had several operations. Her recoveries from these seem to coincide with the seasons, and by spring she always manages to put in a garden. Her complaints about the garden have increased, however, and for the past few summers she has been saying she isn't going to plant vegetables any more.

Last spring we drove up to Vermont later than usual. The day we arrived, I noticed as we passed Blanche's house that her garden hadn't been rototilled yet, let alone planted. This worried me, and the next day I walked down the road to pay her a visit. As I neared the little white house I was relieved to see her begonias in the window boxes. They looked a bit droopy—not as many flowers as usual—but at least they were there. I knocked at the door. It was a while before she answered. When she saw me she smiled and asked me to come inside. She looked much the same, only tired; but when I took her in my arms and gave her a big, careful hug, thinking that she probably didn't get many hugs now that her grandchildren were grown, her body felt as thin and light as a dried stalk.

I took a seat on the sofa, and she perched on the armchair in front of the wall where her favorite snapshots are tacked up. She told me she'd had another operation and had left the hospital only two weeks earlier. One of her friends had planted the begonias in the window box. Her son had taken away the aluminum ladder, not wanting her to go up on the roof any more.

I wasn't sure whether to mention the unplowed vegetable garden, the way one isn't sure whether to refer to a death in the family. Would it be taken as a sign of concern, or cause distress? But she brought it up herself.

"I told them, 'No more garden.' I've been telling them for years it's not worth the bother," she said. I wasn't sure who "they" were—relatives, maybe, or the farmer who dropped by every spring with his rototiller. "You can buy better tomatoes over to Katz's. 'Course they're expensive, but if you add it all up I wouldn't be surprised if they come out cheaper. Why should I have to do it, year after year, with the blackflies? I'll plant grass. Much better." She spoke with satisfaction, as if she'd achieved a lifelong ambition. I thought of how she'd always criticized her beans and squash, the way you might tell your daughter her hair looked better before she cut it, or her dress wasn't becoming—not because you didn't love her but because you did, because you wanted to see her looking as beautiful as you knew she really was.

I made a point of visiting Blanche more often that summer, and when the lady's-slippers bloomed we stood together in the garden, contemplating their perfection. But the bed they were growing in needed weeding.

After a while she said, "I guess you'll wait to dig it until it goes dormant."

"Um," I said, not really paying attention.

"That be the best time, you think?"

It hit me what she was saying. "You mean you want to give me—"

"A shoot," she said quickly. "One of those over there." There were two small divisions she had taken from the main clump at some time in the past and planted at the other end of the bed.

Of course I had sometimes coveted Blanche's lady's-slippers, but now that she had offered me one I felt reluctant to take it. What if I tried to transplant it and it died? What if people thought I'd stolen it from the wild, an act that some would call immoral? But the real reason I hesitated was that I wanted the lady's-slippers to keep right on growing where they were, in the corner between Blanche's house and the garage, forever.

She said, "Take it, I want you to have it." Lightly, her fingers brushed my arm. "Take it," she repeated. So I said that I would. I would be honored.

The Pond

Ever since coming to Vermont I had been noticing ponds. The summer after my mother died I decided to build one.

Ponds are everywhere in the Green Mountain State, not just the large ones that in other parts of the country would be called lakes, but also the small, man-made earth ponds where fish are raised and cattle come to drink. These latter had always struck me as a part of the rural landscape that was pleasing and even magical; I loved the way a green field would suddenly open to cup a bright scrap of reflected sky.

It had never occurred to me that I might create my own pond until I happened upon a wonderful book: *Earth Ponds: The Country Pond Maker's Guide*, by Tim Matson. It was in the waiting room of a psychotherapist I had gone to see during my mother's last illness, a time when I was visiting her at the nursing home every day between my other responsibilities. I picked up the book, which was lying in the middle of a table as if placed there especially for me. The cover photograph showed a country pond in a field, with low hills in the background. It was a serene picture, utterly simple: earth, water, sky. The field and hills were a dull, olive green— not the vibrant green of summer but the darker hue of early fall, just before the foliage kindles into flame. The water reflected a blue sky and a few floating white clouds. I turned the book upside down. The picture looked exactly the same, so perfect was the reflection, except that now the sky had an ominous darkness, as if a storm were on the way.

Not long afterward, my mother died, and in early spring I went up to Vermont, alone. Winter had not yet relaxed its grip on the land, and the days were bleak and cold, with an occasional dusting of snow. Each morning I would build a fire in the Franklin stove and sit for a while, staring into the flames and looking through old papers and photographs. I especially liked a snapshot of my mother taken in her twenties. She is standing on the end of a diving board in a long, flapperish swimsuit and a white rubber bathing cap fastened under her chin. Back arched, arms stretched above her head, palms together, she is about to dive backwards into the pool. Under the taut fabric of the suit, her large, round breasts are flattened in the style of the period. Boyish figures were in vogue, and my mother's proportions were generous. In the picture she is young, strong, and smiling.

When I wasn't sorting old papers I often picked up *Earth Ponds: The Country Pond Maker's Guide*—by then I had acquired my own copy—and leafed through it. I found this activity oddly comforting. After a while I almost knew the book by heart.

Gradually my idle page-turning resulted in a plan. I would build an earth pond that summer, one that would be visible from the house and large enough for swimming—in fact, as big as the terrain and my finances permitted.

Our old blue farmhouse had classic lines, but its relationship to the land around it was uneasy. It perched on a rise in a large, semicircular clearing, half of which was swampland overgrown with brush. There was no comfortable place to sit outdoors, and no room for a garden. I thought the swamp had possibilities. It was right near the house—you could certainly see it—and it was already holding water, or rather mud. Perhaps we could dig a pond there, pile up some of the excavated earth for the dam, and with the rest create level terraces that would give us some usable land.

I found a local farmer who agreed to clear the brush from the swamp, and one morning he came over with a chainsaw and set to work. The job took only a day; the next day he piled the brush into a great pyre and burned it. The farmer owned a small backhoe, and I watched while he dug five test holes. There were cautionary tales in *Earth Ponds* about pond-builders who had omitted this step and ended up with ponds that failed to hold water, due to the wrong kind of soil. A giant crater in my backyard would be no improvement over a swamp.

The earth scooped out by the backhoe was rich and black and as soggy as a wet sponge. Below a deep layer of topsoil was clay. Water began oozing into the holes as soon as the bucket of the backhoe was withdrawn, so I thought things looked promising. Still, the book suggested waiting to make sure the test holes would hold water during dry weather.

The farmer had trouble maneuvering his machine out of the mud, and I had a few problems too, for I'd followed him out into the swamp, sinking in above the ankles with every step. Mom would have been shocked if she could have seen me, for she believed in the importance of dry feet. When I was little she used to scold me for going out in the rain without my galoshes, something I liked to do whenever I could get away with it.

Eventually we reached dry land. The farmer dismounted from his machine and we stood together surveying the holes. I said, "Do you think they'll hold water?"

The corners of his lips twitched. "Might have trouble keeping it out."

Friends told me the local Soil Conservation Service offered free advice about pond-building. It was pretty much a one-man agency due to budget cuts, they said, but the man in charge, Tom Maclay, knew a lot about ponds.

After several calls—busy, he said, not enough staff— he stopped by one day in June, a stalwart, white-haired Yankee wearing khaki pants and a nylon windbreaker. "Dug your test holes already, I see," he said approvingly. He walked around inspecting the site as I trailed after him, staying a few feet back not only as a sign of respect but also because it was hard to keep up with him. "Should make a good pond," he said finally. "But there's no guarantees. Feller I know dug a pond that looked fine until it sprung a leak. Water drained out overnight. I went over and took a look at it but—" He shook his head. "Ledge underneath had a crack in it. Course he could have tried lining it with bentonite but—whew! that's pricey stuff! And you can bust the seal."

This was daunting. Still, Tom assured me, my swamp looked like a good site for a pond. He started talking about watersheds and runoff and pond-feet, terms familiar to me from the book though I couldn't follow his calculations. Scanning the hill behind the swamp, he estimated that six to eight acres of upland would drain into the pond.

I had no idea at the time how important Tom Maclay was to become in my Vermont life as helper, teacher, and friend, but right from the start I trusted him. He treated me like a collaborator, and the fact that I was a woman didn't seem to bother him a bit. He went to his pickup truck and came back with a long white measuring stick marked off in feet, which he handed me. I held it upright in various locations while he sighted at it from a distance.

"Okay," he said finally. "We'll put the pond here. It'll be a nice size, about an eighth of an acre—say a hundred feet the long way." The contractor he liked to work with was DuBois, which he pronounced "DOO-boys." You could get the work done cheaper, he said, but DuBois would do it right.

It hit me that this pond was really going to happen. I could still say "No," or tell Tom I would think it over; but I didn't want to, even if it felt like hubris to make such a large mark—100 feet!—on a landscape I didn't really know.

I said, "When can we start?"

A backhoe and a bulldozer would be needed, he said, and it wouldn't pay for DuBois to truck in the machines for a small job like mine. But in three or four weeks they had to do roadwork in the neighborhood, and he thought they could fit my job around it if he talked to them. Until then I would have to wait.

Waiting is something I don't do well. My mother, too, hated to wait, and "Hurry up!" was one of the great, overarching commandments of my childhood. It issued not only from her but from grandparents and aunts and uncles, all the time. Work hard, work fast, and get the job done: these would have been the words on our family crest, if we'd had one, and they'd sunk into my bones.

In some ways this had been a blessing. Getting things done, all sorts of things, had been a source of enormous satisfaction in my life and had benefitted others as well. But it had also been a burden. A continual self-flagellation goes on, invisibly, in people who are noted for getting things done. Our projects may begin in a surge of joyful creativity, but carrying them through to completion, against the drag of our own laziness, eventually requires that inner, invisible whip. It's what urges us onward, even when we love the things we are doing. Or we love having done them. The lash also falls on the people around us, when we need help in carrying out our grand designs.

Psychotherapy has unflattering names for such qualities. Obsessive-compulsive is one. But therapy doesn't provide a cure, whatever the profession may claim, for these are not really disorders but character traits, at least until they reach the extremity of compulsive handwashing, or inability to sleep unless one has taken off one's clothing in a certain order, or other such torments. Therapy can help us understand these traits better and learn to live with them—that's all.

There was nothing I could do to get the pond under way any faster. So I told myself to be patient and tried to go about my usual activities. I kept gravitating, though, toward the old sofa in front of the window overlooking the swamp, where I would stare outside, trying to visualize where the pond would go, what the dam would look like, and how the land around the house should be graded. The pond possessed me, and after a while I resigned myself to that fact. I took more books about pond-building out of the library and read them obsessively, although *Earth Ponds* remained my bible.

And I thought about my mother. Mostly my thoughts kept returning to her last years, the period of her illness and death. Long ago I had come to terms with the mother of my childhood, a young, divorced woman trying to raise an only child. But I hadn't yet gotten over losing the old mother, and perhaps I never would.

Mom used to tell people I'd saved her life. She was talking about what had happened when she was sixty-nine and living in the Florida retirement community to which she'd just moved following the death of Dudley, my stepfather. Her illness came on suddenly. One day she was hanging pictures on her walls, swimming in the pool, and playing bridge in the community house with her new neighbors, and the next she was lying on the floor of her bedroom, trying to crawl to the telephone.

She couldn't make it. She would have lain there until she died if a neighbor hadn't noticed her absence and looked in the window.

I got a call from her doctor and flew down to Florida. I found my mother in a tiny community hospital, drifting in and out of consciousness. Her doctor didn't know what was wrong with her. It wasn't her heart: that organ had been pumping away faithfully ever since a successful surgery three years earlier, and you could hear a faint click-clicking of the artificial valve if you listened closely.

It was the Fourth of July, and a skeleton crew was on duty at the hospital. The laboratory was closed for the weekend; all tests would have to wait until it reopened on Tuesday. Mother was on oxygen, but although the tank in her room hissed, I noticed that the tube lay open on her chest. Maybe the nurse had forgotten to insert it in her nostrils. Maybe it had fallen out.

After that I sat by her bed for two days. There was no one to spell me, no one to call, for I had no sisters or brothers and my husband was traveling in Europe. I'd left the boys with a neighbor, and Anne, my youngest, then seven, was away for the first time at camp. A whole new life was about to start for me and Joe now that all the children were in school, a life with quiet times for the two of us, and plenty of time for me to write. Or so we imagined.

Now and then the doctor came by, looking flustered, as Mother sank deeper toward unconsciousness. She was in terrible pain. There was still no diagnosis, let alone treatment, and the doctor started hinting that I should prepare myself for the worst.

This came as a tremendous shock. My mother was a woman of great vitality, and it hadn't occurred to me that she might not get well. It was simply a question of find-ing out what was wrong and giving her the appropriate treatment. The realization that her doctor thought Mom was dying jolted me out of my passivity. Why was I sitting by the bed like an idiot? I had to get her out of there!

I can't recall how many telephone calls it took. I do remember shrieking at the woman in Medical Records, demanding my mother's X-rays so I could hand-carry them to the big teaching hospital I'd persuaded to admit her. No, I would not let the hospital send them over according to standard procedure, whenever they happened to get around to it! I would sue everyone in sight! I would sue the hospital, sue the doctor, sue her personally if she didn't produce those X-rays! I would come behind the counter and grab them off the shelf myself—did she think I couldn't figure out an alphabetical filing system?

I don't know why she didn't call security—maybe the guard was off celebrating the Fourth—but when the ambulance came and I climbed inside, the X-rays were clutched firmly in my hand. As we sped along, siren wailing, I held my mother's hand and winced every time we went over a bump and she moaned in her stupor.

At the new hospital she was diagnosed quickly. Multiple myeloma, the resident said, showing me the tiny, tell-tale pits in the X-rays of her skull. It was a cancer of the blood, in which calcium leaches out of the bones, causing multiple fractures and excruciating pain. The calcium accumulates in the blood, rapidly causing stupor and then coma and death. Her condition was grave. They would start her on chemotherapy immediately.

After I talked to the resident I went to the waiting room and hunted up a telephone. I called an architect I knew in Maryland and asked him to draw plans for an addition to our house—a large room for my mother, with a bathroom and kitchenette. The doorways were to be wide enough for a wheelchair, and all the electric outlets should be placed at table height where an invalid could reach them. I told him where to find a key to the house so he could go in and make measurements, and I asked him to line up a contractor.

All this was an act of faith. My mother was not going to die—I refused to consider the possibility.

Ten days later her condition had improved enough for me to take her back with me to Maryland, where a long period of treatment and convalescence followed. When I got home I looked up multiple myeloma in a medical encyclopedia, where it was described as "a fatal disease." Fortunately I didn't know this while she was in the hospital, or I might have let her die. Instead she recovered. Or maybe she went into a remission that lasted until she died seven years later of something else—which amounts to the same thing, as far as I'm concerned.

Seven years. It doesn't seem much, as I write the words. Do seven years really make such a difference, are they worth all the trouble that came with them?

Yes! Absolutely! Five of those years were wonderful—they were the time of my mother's radiant, final flowering. She reveled in those years, and I wouldn't have missed them for anything.

One morning about a month after Tom's visit, a rumbling awakened me. I got up and looked out the window. All I could see was a dense fog with a thickening where the four ancient sugar maples stood, shielding the house from the road. The rumbling continued—"Brroom, brroom"—so I got dressed and went to investigate. A huge flatbed truck loomed out of the mist. It was parked by the side of the road, and a yellow backhoe on caterpillar treads was inching its way down the ramp in back. Compared to this monster, the backhoe that had dug the test holes had been a toy. I waited until the unloading was complete and then went over and talked to the operator. He was in his twenties and had an open, country face and one earring. He told me his name was Andre.

I offered to show him the site, but he declined politely. Tom would show him, he said. I offered him coffee, but he'd brought some along in a cardboard cup from the Stop 'N Shop.

A few minutes later a pickup truck drove up and an elderly man in immaculate work clothes got out stiffly. This was Mr. DuBois himself, the senior Mr. DuBois, who had recently retired in favor of his son, he informed me. "Ma'am," he said as he shook my hand, "It's gonna be a big mess."

"That's all right. I'm expecting it."

"*Big* mess. Long as you know. Now, you're gonna be the foreman." He peered at me under heavy eyebrows and I detected a twinkle.

"I am? Then I'd like to save the rhubarb. There's an old patch on the edge of the swamp."

Mr. DuBois went over to the backhoe, where Andre was still sitting in the cab drinking his coffee. "Andre, this nice lady says she'll bake you a rhubarb pie if you save her rhubarb. Think you can do it?"

"Yep."

"Says he can do it." Mr. DuBois shook my hand again. "Gotta run over the dentist, get some stitches out. My gums are receding. Aaah, I'm an old man. I'm falling apart." He climbed back in his truck and revved up the motor. "Big mess, remember!" With a wave of his hand he was gone.

Moments later, Tom drove up. He greeted me, exchanged a few words with Andre, and the two strode off in the direction of the swamp in their big, olive-green rubber boots with yellow laces. I trailed after them.

They surveyed the area gloomily. By now the mist had thinned. Andre said, "Awful wet."

Tom nodded. "Gotta pile it."

Both men folded their arms across their chests. Andre said, "Might have to finish it next year."

"Maybe this fall."

"If it don't rain."

They headed back toward the driveway. The inspection was over.

Tom explained to me that the swamp was so saturated with water that the pond would have to be dug in two stages. Otherwise the machines would keep getting stuck in the mud. First the backhoe would scoop out as much swamp muck as possible, using the bucket at the end of its long arm while the machine remained on dry land. This muck—rich, black topsoil that could be used for the new lawn we were planning—would be piled and left to dry out. Some of the hardpan would also be dug out and piled separately. Then a ditch would be cut for drainage. There was no telling how soon the area would be dry enough for the backhoe to return, together with a bulldozer to shape the basin and build the dam. Fall was the driest period of the year, and it was possible the pond could be completed at that time. If not, we'd have to wait until next summer.

More waiting. "And today? That's it for today?"

"Oh, no, today we start digging."

It took a day and a half. Over and over, the arm of the backhoe swung out into the swamp, lifted a dripping bucketful of mud, and pivoted to deposit it on dry land. Then the backhoe would move a few yards and resume digging. I watched, hypnotized—first standing outside, and then through the window when the stench, and the bites of the black flies that rose in swarms from the disturbed muck, got to be too much for me. Tom stood on the edge of the swamp. He didn't seem to be doing much. Now and then he raised an arm and pointed, or walked some distance away and sighted through a small instrument, or exchanged a few words with Andre.

The piles grew longer and higher, and soon the tracks of the machine were everywhere. During a brief pause Andre dug up the rhubarb and trundled it over to a level spot near the driveway. I separated the clump into six nice divisions and planted them three feet apart so they would have room to spread. Next year I would bake a rhubarb pie.

As the digging proceeded, the backhoe started pulling giant stones out of the earth. It was exciting to see them, and every time one emerged I would run out of the house yelling, "Save that stone! I want that stone!" They could be used to make a rock garden that would also serve as a retaining wall. Obligingly, Andre set them aside in a separate pile.

By mid-afternoon of the second day the work was done. Andre loaded the backhoe onto the flatbed truck and departed. Tom said there was nothing more he could do for now. The soil would have to drain into the trench made by the backhoe, which emptied into the ditch at the side of the road. He didn't know how long that would take. He'd stop by in the fall to check. His last words, as he swung himself up into his pickup truck, were: "Pray for a dry summer!"

Ponds were everywhere that summer. As I drove around the countryside I kept slowing down to study them. Hmm, this one had an island in the middle, while that one had a double row of young pines, planted to screen it from the road. A family of ducks paddled charmingly across another.

One day I noticed a young woman squatting on her haunches in a field beside a house. She was staring down into a huge, raw hole in the ground. I pulled into the driveway and walked over to her as she looked up, startled.

"Hi, did you just dig a pond?" I asked her, although she was a perfect stranger. "We're digging one, too."

"Uh huh." She could hardly deny it.

"What are you doing?" I sounded like a six-year-old.

"Watching it fill."

"Can I watch, too?"

"I guess so."

I moved a little closer. I could tell she wasn't in the mood for conversation.

We stared into the hole. There was a puddle way down in the bottom, and a shiny, crooked line that might have been a trickle of water. The puddle didn't seem to be getting any bigger. Still, after a while I noticed a white pebble gradually become submerged in water.

The woman's pond was filling awfully slowly. At this rate the water would take weeks or months to reach the top of the bank. I didn't point this out to her; I didn't want to insult her pond. She was bonding with it, and the slowness of the process didn't seem to bother her. It occurred to me that maybe it didn't matter how long it took, a thought my mother would have found heretical.

While I waited for the piles of swamp mud to dry, I made plans for the rock garden. It wouldn't be a real rock garden, I decided after reading a couple of books on the subject. I wasn't going to plant tiny, choice alpine plants. The landscape was too large, and they sounded too hard to grow. I'd taken a few steps toward becoming a gardener by now, and I knew I'd never be the kind who enjoys fussing over rarities. I liked the tough, hardy, free-flowering perennials that flourished in Vermont's short growing season. I would plant common things like daylilies and phlox, oriental poppies and irises, shasta daisies and perennial geraniums.

My mother had been a nature-lover too, but animals interested her more than plants. She considered gardening a waste of time. Sometimes she would go out in my grandparents' garden with shears in her hand and do a bit of clipping—I wouldn't call it pruning. Even before I knew anything about gardening I used to wince when she attacked a shrub. She just hacked. She had no feeling for the way the thing wanted to grow.

Fortunately for me, her method of child-rearing wasn't quite so drastic, even though she was strict and could be stern, to the point that my friends were rather afraid of her—except when she told jokes, which happened pretty often. Some of my mother's jokes were risqué; these she reserved for grownups. Usually my mother sensed the way I wanted to grow, and did what she could to encourage me.

I've thought many times about something she said a few days after her stroke, two years before she died. The doctors had not yet been able to stop the bleeding in her head, and as I sat beside her hospital bed, more and more of her brain cells were dying. Most of the time she lay mute, or muttered a few words that made no sense; but a moment came when she suddenly looked at me with calm recognition. "Someday you'll write about this," she said. And with the half of her face that wasn't paralyzed, she smiled.

I have always been grateful for these words, her last gift to me. Only love could have given her the strength to say them, for by then love was all she had left. They told me she accepted me as I was. That she really knew me. They freed me, finally, to write—yes, even about her.

Fifteen years have gone by since the day my mother had her stroke. My mind slides down the burned-in grooves of these memories all too easily. I was standing outside our Maryland house when the large, shiny American car pulled into the driveway. I can still see the three white-haired heads of the women inside. My mother, in the passenger seat, was much the shortest, for she'd lost several inches when the multiple myeloma had compressed her spine. For the last five years she'd seemed well. She'd even been able to move out of our house into her own apartment a few blocks away.

That day she'd been playing bridge with some of the many friends she'd made since coming to Maryland. The day before she'd been reorganizing the catalogue at the town library, and the following day she was to be at her post in the Red Cross bloodmobile, handing out orange juice and cookies. Mom had become so well known in town that people had started saying to me, "Oh, you must be Shirley Bryant's daughter." It took me aback—after all, I'd been the editor of the local newspaper—but tickled me, too. "What a gal!" I would say to myself. "What a role model!"

When the car drove up I hurried over to it. I hadn't been expecting to see my mother until the weekend. One of Mom's friends got out and said to me, "She dropped her cards."

She'd dropped them on the table. They'd slipped right out of her hand. The friends had thought they'd better bring her to my house.

They knew perfectly well what was happening. These were very intelligent old women, sharp bridge players. And I knew what was happening, too. Instantly.

We looked at each other—all of us except my mother, whose head was lolling. We helped her out of the car, onto the porch, and into a chair beside the front door. She couldn't sit straight and I had to hold her up. Her eyes had a distant look. I shouted for my husband, who came running from the house. Mother's friends got back in the car and left. I told him, "She's having a stroke! Call an ambulance!"

He said, "What's the number? How do you know it's a stroke? Are you sure?" Her body was jerking. She was having a seizure. I had to hold on to her.

Our son appeared and I cried, "Hold her!"

He grabbed her and I ran inside as my husband followed me, leaking questions: "Are you sure it's a stroke? Shouldn't she lie down? Don't you think we should bring her in?" He couldn't absorb it.

I pounced on the Yellow Pages, screaming, "Shut up! Shut up!" crumpling the pages, trying to find the number of the ambulance service, unable to think with all that noise.

I wish I could forget these details, but the memories just won't fade. I keep feeling that I should have been able to do more. I should have been able to save her.

✢

It was a dry summer, for Vermont.

I watched the stinking piles of mud steam in the sunlight, and I waited. I started wondering if Tom had forgotten me. He'd built more than two hundred and fifty ponds—"I gave up counting," he'd told me—so what was one more, and a "small job" at that? I restrained myself from calling him. He struck me as a man who didn't need nagging.

On the third Monday of August he showed up unannounced. We walked out to the swamp, and he climbed the piles and stomped them with his feet. "Dry enough," he announced when he came down. "We start tomorrow."

✢

All that week and into the next, the earth moved. The noise of the backhoe made the air vibrate and the windows rattle. When the hole reached a certain size, the backhoe trundled into it and continued digging until the pond was the right depth—eleven feet at the deepest point. From my vantage point at the window, I could see only the tireless arm reaching up over the edge of the hole to dump its load.

A bulldozer arrived and Buddy, the operator, began to push the piles of earth where they were needed, spreading and compacting them. Often the bulldozer would be on the verge of toppling into the hole, and the backhoe would come to the rescue, pushing the other machine back from the brink with its powerful arm. The slope of the sides was steep, as shallow ponds were apt to silt up quickly and become clogged with cattails, Tom told me. When I replied, "I don't have to plant cattails," he laughed. Cattails didn't need to be planted. They appeared whether you wanted them or not, for they grew in the local wetlands and released millions of almost invisibly fine seeds that floated on the breeze and took root whenever they happened to land in shallow water.

A bundle of two-inch iron pipes arrived, and when the excavation was deep enough Tom and Andre coupled the sections together and laid a long drainpipe in place. The pond would be, in effect, like a giant bathtub. Water would flow in from springs, and once it reached a certain level a six-inch spillway near the top of the dam would carry off the overflow. To empty the pond for cleaning, all we had to do was remove the stopper in the drainpipe.

The weather remained dry and sunny and the men worked from seven in the morning until four in the afternoon, piling earth for the dams, packing the clay with the bulldozers until it was almost as hard as cement, and coordinating their machines in a well-practiced pas de deux. There was a timelessness to their motions now, a hypnotic rhythm to the repetitive spreading and smoothing and packing.

And then—suddenly, it seemed—the job was done. The pond was finished. I felt a moment of regret. By now we had all become friends. Buddy, the bulldozer operator, had confided in me the details of his recent surgery to remove a kidney. The doctor had advised him to find another job, he said, to avoid the constant vibration from the machine. But he liked his work and was good at it, so he figured he'd take his chances.

After the men had left, I walked out on the dam and surveyed the barren moonscape. At the bottom of the crater, water was seeping from a spring. More water flowed from a second spring at the edge of the woods. Where there was water there would be life. Yet the pond had not begun to fill, for the drainpipe was still carrying off the water as fast as it flowed in. A puddle had collected in the bottom—that was all.

Suddenly the corner of my eye caught a flicker of motion. What was that? Something in the puddle? A fish? It couldn't be. Carefully, I picked my way down to the bottom of the crater. Peering into the puddle I saw a frog, swimming around in four inches of water as if he were really enjoying himself. I stood there, marveling. Already life had come to the pond, and I hadn't had to do a thing.

I climbed back up the slope, and when I reached the top I was smiling. I was remembering something that had happened when I was twelve. That year, Mom and I spent the winter with my grandparents in Hollywood, Florida. She used to take me to the beach, where we would collect shells, exclaiming over their colors. But when we took the shells home the colors quickly faded. Trying to brighten them, I put some in a glass jar and filled it with water. I set the jar outside the door and forgot about it.

About a week later I looked in the jar and saw tiny, threadlike creatures swimming in the water. I was astounded. Where had they come from? Were they fish? There must have been eggs stuck to the shells—something like that. I watched the creatures, delighted with their wriggling motion as they rose to the surface of the water and plunged down again. So pretty! I called my mother to come and see.

"Well, will you look at that!" she said. She was then in her late thirties, buxom and still quite beautiful, and was probably wearing one of the sun-bleached cotton playsuits she favored that year, ironing a fresh one each morning. She squatted down beside me and studied the creatures more closely. Her face changed. "Uh oh."

"What is it? What are they?"

"Mosquitoes."

"Mosquitoes?"

"Mosquito larvae." We looked at each other and started to laugh. Every time we stopped we would start again. Mom poured out the water. She showed me an article in the *Hollywood Sun Tattler* that said mosquitoes could breed even in small amounts of water—rainwater in discarded rubber tires was mentioned. An editorial called on readers to check their property for standing water and get rid of it.

So like good citizens, we inspected my grandparents' yard and poured out the rainwater that had collected here and there in pails and flowerpot saucers. As we walked my mother explained the difference between aedes and anopheles mosquitoes, and how the latter transmitted malaria; this led to talk of the building of the Panama Canal and the amazing way canal locks worked, and no doubt other things as well. Mom, my first teacher, who loved nature and liked to know exactly how things worked.

When I'd made a complete circuit of the pond, I went in the house and baked two loaf cakes. Tomorrow I would give one to Andre and the other to Buddy. For Tom I'd already made a jar of apple jelly, using apples from the old tree that grew near the edge of the pond. Before the brush had been cleared away, I hadn't even noticed that it was an apple tree. Tom had spotted it right away and made sure to save it.

As soon as we had a stopper for the drainpipe, the pond could begin to fill. "What you want is a nice piece of cedar," Tom said. "Cedar isn't going to rot on you." There was a fellow who knew how to make cedar plugs for ponds. Tom would see how busy he was.

More waiting. I felt an urge to say, "What's wrong with plastic?" But I restrained myself.

This time the waiting seemed interminable. A firestorm of goldenrod raged across the fields, Labor Day came and went, and the sugar maples unfurled their first red flags, warning that soon I would have to return to Maryland. My husband took the suitcases down from the attic and, halfheartedly, I began to pack.

A couple of days later, Tom and his young grandson, Kevin, drove up in the pickup truck. "Been waiting for this?" said Tom, handing me the plug with a flourish. It was about eight inches long, smelled of pinewoods, and had been turned on a lathe like an old-fashioned chair rail. I ran to get my camera. The picture I snapped shows Tom with his hand on Kevin's shoulder; Kevin, holding the plug, has a big, gap-toothed grin.

For the last time, Tom climbed down to the bottom of the excavation. He hammered the stopper into the drainpipe. In the quiet country air, the blows rang out like the sound of a bell. When he climbed back up again, we shook hands. "The baby she is born!" he said, and even though he'd built hundreds of ponds, he seemed as pleased as I was. For a while we stood side by side without speaking, watching the pond begin to fill. By the time Tom and Kevin left, the puddle at the bottom had doubled in size.

Watching the pond fill, I had plenty of time to think. My mother's life had come to an end the day she had her stroke. Half-paralyzed, incontinent, and functioning mentally on a very low level, she'd continued to exist for another two years but was no longer the same person. The extent of her brain damage made recovery impossible. Yet she retained enough awareness to be miserable in the nursing home, and sometimes from halfway down the hall I would hear her raging at the aides. One time I entered her room just as she'd managed to shove her tray on the floor, and I saw the food splatter in every direction.

We waited for the ordeal to end, two women not greatly gifted with patience. I visited as often as I could bear.

"What would I do without you?" she whispered once, as I put my arm around her and gave her a kiss.

"I don't do anything for you." It was true. My inability to help her galled me terribly. But I hope she felt my love.

After two years in the nursing home, she developed pneumonia, which used to be called "the old man's friend." Soon she sank into a coma. I started spending the whole day in her room, bringing a tote bag full of work to do while I waited: bills to pay, bank statements to review, tasks requiring little concentration. While I worked, the nurses and aides came in and out, checking her temperature and blood pressure, changing her linens—doing whatever they had to do. I paid no particular attention.

On the third day of her coma a nurse came in with a medicine cart. She took out a syringe and filled it.

"What's that you're giving her?" I said.

"An antibiotic."

"An antibiotic? Why? What for?"

"Doctor's orders."

I couldn't believe what was happening. Mom's body was doing its best to die, and the nursing home was trying to prevent it! I said, "Oh no, I'm very sorry but you're not giving her an antibiotic. What on earth is the point?" I was trembling.

"She needs it. She has pneumonia."

"She does not need it." Mom didn't want to live—this I knew. After my stepfather died, she'd made me swear that if she ever became hopelessly ill I would not let her life be prolonged. She'd even written me a letter of instructions, only I wasn't sure where I'd put it.

Now the time had come to honor my word, but the promise had been easier to make than to keep.

I got up and went over to the nurse. "No antibiotics!" I said.

"It's not up to me. I have to follow the doctor's orders."

"You are not going to give her that shot."

We glared at each other. Finally she turned away. "Well, it's your responsibility!"

"Yes, it's my responsibility."

The doctor, a nice man I'd known for years, showed up about an hour later. After we talked, he reluctantly agreed to discontinue the antibiotic. He wrote in the order book, "Patient's family refuses medication," and asked me to initial it.

My mother died the next day. I'd gone out for a short walk, so I wasn't with her at the moment of her death. I wish I had been, but I doubt she knew.

After her death I found the letter and gave it to the doctor to read. It said:

To my dearest daughter, Dorothy—

I have seen Dudley suffer horribly for weeks. Even though his condition was terminal, and hopeless, he was kept alive to suffer even more. There was no dignity in his death and his last days were degrading to him and to those of us who watched him.

Therefore, Dorothy, I beg of you—and this is my final request—

Should I become hopelessly ill but can survive indefinitely on machines, even with a poor prognosis, please see to it that the machines are not used. Or if they have been started, I want them discontinued. I want no special medical procedures or any medical procedures if my condition is hopeless for a normal existence. Let me go to sleep—please!

This is my wish and I rely on you to see that my wishes are carried out.

Love,
Mother (Shirley Bryant)

The doctor said, "I'm glad you showed me this," and started to cry. She'd been his patient since she'd come to live with me, and he had liked her.

I felt as if I had killed her. It's no use saying it doesn't bother me. But as long as I had to do it, I wish I could have done it sooner and spared her those two terrible years. And when the time comes, I hope one of my children will do it for me.

I wish my mother could have seen the pond. She'd have loved the darting dragonflies, the frogs, the bats that circle the water at twilight, and the ducks that use the pond as a stopover on their migrations. She'd have fed the koi, the multicolored Japanese carp with which the pond is stocked, and which can live a hundred years. In Japan they are revered as symbols of longevity and wisdom.

Except during prolonged hot spells, rare in Vermont, our pond is very cold, for it is fed by deep springs. I find it extraordinarily refreshing. I have to immerse myself gradually at first, but then I launch off from the dock, gasping, and swim away. I prefer a slow, easy sidestroke that barely ruffles the surface of the water.

Usually the koi come over to keep me company. They like to swim in a school and pay me the honor of including me. Some of them are over a foot long, with stout bodies, and I can understand why certain of my guests are a little afraid of them. I've read that koi can grow to a length of two or three feet, which even I find a daunting prospect. But they never bite, although like all carp they are quite voracious.

When I'm very tired, or hot, or tense, or in a bad mood, I find that a swim in those amniotic waters cures all my ills for a while. As I glide through the cool, silken water, play with the fish, and gaze at the flowers that grow on the bank, my cares slip away, my mind empties itself, I'm washed clean of my sins, and I become as innocent of grief as a newborn child.

The Daffodil Border

Although she died two years ago, Wanda welcomed me on my return to Vermont as I had known she would, out in the meadow where the path swings around to run alongside the ditch. The daffodil border was at its peak, the yellow and white flowers bobbing as a chill wind swept through them like a rough caress; and there was Wanda in my head with her urchin grin and whiskey voice saying, "So, Kiddo, what do you think? You like?" As if my not liking that sweep of spring splendor, her last gift to me, could possibly be in question.

"Oh, I love that white one especially."

The white daffodils were the cleanest of whites, without a ghost of yellow on petals or cup, as white as Wanda's hair, which I used to try to talk her into dyeing. After all she was not yet forty, twenty years younger than I, and she so keenly hungered for a man, so desperately missed sex, which she'd had a lot of, and a man's protectiveness, which she'd seldom known, so why not dye her hair? Maybe the white hair put men off, made them think of their mothers or something. "Men are weird," I would say, or she would say—it was a recurring theme of our conversations.

Yet Wanda did look older than her years (this of course I did not say), because her face was creased and weatherbeaten from outdoor work. Her body, though, was supple, firm, and strong, her breasts high, her freckled arms and legs slim. Youthful and perfect her body seemed when we swam with the fish in my icy pond to wash off the sweat from gardening. If she complained now and then about her back or remarked that she'd made another appointment with the osteopath, why, she was a gardener after all, always digging and stooping and hauling. It made perfect sense that her back should hurt.

I always used to feel a twinge of guilt when Wanda's back hurt, because she was my gardener, and deep down I didn't believe it was right for me to have a gardener. It was my garden and therefore I should do the work, all of it. I should be the one with the backache, because I didn't come from the kind of people who had gardeners, or land rather than yards, or maybe not even yards but just fire escapes and a couple of flowerpots. Who did I think I was? People with gardeners were the idle rich, parasites living off the sweat of the masses. It was my backache Wanda was having.

Still I continued to employ her, because I had more garden than I could manage, and she needed the money. After all, she was a gardener. It was her profession.

Wanda maintained a personal relationship with the plants under her care. To the weaklings she would croon encouragingly, "Come on, you can do it, Buddy," leaning over so that her head almost touched their leaves. Plants that were flourishing and full of bloom she praised to their faces, saying, "Well, look at you!" She was dismayed when I threatened to throw the clematis on the compost heap because it had barely produced a flower in five years, although I had transplanted it twice, trying to find a place where it would be happy. "Give it a chance," she pleaded. "Leave the poor thing alone. It has to get used to a spot before blooming."

Still, she frowned on unnecessary coddling "Treat 'em rough!" she would tell me, as I carefully sawed through the rootball of a perennial with a knife from the kitchen. "Give it a whack!" And throwing the clump on the ground, she would quarter the rootball with three swift blows of her spade.

Wanda's ire was reserved for weeds, which she called "vicious," especially after they had attained a good size. "Ah, a Vicious Weed!" she would cry—or simply a "V.W."— as we walked around the flower beds together, discussing what to do next. Then she would reach behind her for the short-handled weeder worn in the belt of her jeans and pounce on the offender.

In the winters Wanda worked in Key West as a waitress. Long ago, she told me, she'd been some sort of social worker—occasionally she would talk about maybe going back to school and getting her degree. In her early years in Vermont she'd birthed the babies of the hippie community on East Hill, of which she'd been one of the founding members. I could see Wanda in all of these roles. As a social worker I imagined her counseling alcoholics or druggies. I could see her as a waitress especially because, despite a deep vein of shyness, she sometimes

had the look and manner of a tough, wisecracking waitress in a Hollywood movie, the kind the men referred to
as a "dame."

Because Wanda was both employee and friend, at
times our relationship was tricky; but mostly it felt simple
and natural, if a bit feudal. Once when I had a cousins' re-
union she cooked for me, arranging the platters beauti-
fully and decorating them with edible flowers; afterward
she cleared up and washed the dishes. But at most of my
parties she was a guest, sometimes seeming ill at ease as if
in need of a few stiff drinks to relax her, and other times
smiling and talking and just having a good time.

I had the bigger house, with land and gardens spread
about it; she referred to her house as "the shack," though
it had its gardens, naturally, which she'd created in part
from the cast-off plants of her employers and friends. I
had a husband of many years; she'd had liaisons of varying lengths, one of which had produced her two children, teenagers when I first met her. In short, I had all
the material things she lacked: savings, a reliable car, insurance against every calamity one could imagine. But
Wanda was proud, and only once or twice asked for a
small loan, which I was to deduct from her pay; this I did
while wondering what she was living on. I thought it
showed a noble spirit that she seemed to like me anyway.

Sometimes it seemed that the shakiness of Wanda's
finances worried me more than it did her. She used to
bring me plants and refuse to accept payment. I would
tell her, "You'll never get rich at this rate, Wanda," and
try to talk her into starting a small nursery business on
the side, to supply her employers with perennials. She
had enough land, and there were always excess plants

when the gardens in which she worked became over-grown. Instead of throwing some of the spare divisions on the compost heap, she ought to take them home, plant them, and later resell them. If she charged a dollar or two less than the prices at the local nurseries she could have a nice little supplement to her income. It would be a good deal all around. "I'm your business manager," I would say, "You should listen to me." But she would shake her head and insist she could never charge her clients for plants. Perhaps she was simply too tired after work to summon the energy. Perhaps some perversity in her nature found the idea of living without money worries disturbing.

Once when she was having persistent car problems that left her with no way of getting to work, I offered to give her a car that was sitting on my driveway back in Maryland. It was an elderly gas-guzzler, but very reliable. The offer precipitated a crisis. For several days she didn't say yes or no, but acted sullen, withdrawn, and suspicious. I'd never seen her like that before. Finally she said, "Look, we have to talk. If you, like, give me the car, what does it mean? What happens after that? You know, I have to have my independence."

"Of course you do."

"Just because you give me a car doesn't mean I don't have my own life."

"Wanda, all it means is you need a car, and I have a car I don't need. So take it. It doesn't mean you have to be my slave. Nothing will change."

Something did change though, but subtly. We became closer and the level of trust between us deepened. I think it was the talking more than the car that did it.

I bought her a ticket and put her on the train to Washington, and my husband met her at Union Station. He had taken the car to the garage so it would be in shape for an eleven-hour trip. When Wanda returned with the car she told me that she'd been scared of driving it all the way back to Vermont. This amazed me, not because I'd have felt any differently, but because she'd been on her own for so long and seemed so physically daring and so used to living on the edge that I'd assumed she must be a fearless driver. She wasn't. I'd just been taken in by the image she tried to present to the world of Wanda the Strong.

The winter before she died I went down to Florida on the Autotrain with my car and ended up stranded in Miami when plans I'd made fell through. Feeling let down and in need of comfort, I was in no mood to get right back on the train and head north. I remembered that Wanda was waitressing in Key West and hunted up the nearest telephone. Then I hesitated. Calling her seemed a bold step, not only because I'd never spoken to her before in the winter (we'd exchanged a few letters), but because if I called, the balance of power would shift. This time she would be the one who could give or withhold, and I would be the needy one. I called anyway.

"Come," she said right away. I could sleep on the couch in the room she rented. She didn't think the woman who owned the house would mind. But I had to understand that I'd be on my own, because she had to work. We'd see each other after she got home. Having no car, she commuted by bicycle and was usually very tired when she got home. Maybe the manager would give her a day off.

It was almost midnight when I found the little yellow house where she was living, and although there were cars and pickups all over the front yard, a space had been left near the front door for me to park. Wanda was waiting for me, and after a big hug she took me into the kitchen and introduced me to her landlady, Jane, who said huskily, "Any friend of Wanda's," and shook my hand hard. She was a hale old woman dressed only in a T-shirt that reached to mid-thigh. She'd been drinking beer in the kitchen with her boyfriend, Bradleigh, who was twenty years younger and referred to her as "Cap'n Jane" when he spoke at all. Bradleigh gave me a wave and went back to the fishing rod he'd been repairing. Everyone had stayed up waiting for me, but they all had to get up early, Wanda to serve breakfast at the restaurant and the others to go out in the boat. Cap'n Jane took fishermen out for the day, and when she didn't have any customers she and Bradleigh went out fishing anyway.

Wanda's room, originally a sun porch, was small and, due to the jalousie windows on two walls, pleasantly breezy. She'd made up the couch and insisted on sleeping there, giving me the bed. I was too tired to offer much resistance. We soon fell asleep, but not before she'd told me the love story of Cap'n Jane and Bradleigh.

It had started at the bar in the marina, where they'd fallen into casual conversation one evening. Bradleigh was a West Virginian who'd come down to the Keys to fish. "He was sleeping in his truck," Wanda said disapprovingly. "He wasn't even staying in a motel." Cap'n

Jane had had a bit too much to drink, so Bradleigh had driven her home. When they reached the house he'd helped her inside, and he'd never left.

"That was four months ago." Wanda shook her head. "Don't ask me what he's good for," she added. "Jane's seventy years old and she's a very intelligent person. She really is, she used to be a teacher. But she says she just can't stand not having a man around."

I stayed a week. The days fell into a pleasant if lonely rhythm. I went sightseeing, sketched, and lay on the beach. Downtown the store windows were papered with notices warning of AIDS, and signs urged shoppers to take a handful of condoms from the bowls placed near the cash registers. Wanda told me she was volunteering a few hours a week at an AIDS clinic, and in her letters to her daughter she always enclosed some of the free condoms.

At the back of Cap'n Jane's house, a screened porch overlooked a bamboo-enclosed backyard just big enough to hold a small swimming pool where leaves and struggling insects floated. I swam slow laps there after breakfast, idly studying the narrow border of vegetation—you could hardly call it a garden, clearly neither Wanda nor anyone else paid any attention to it—and wondering how it would be to live in Key West.

On the morning after my arrival while I was taking a dip in the pool, a half-naked young man emerged from a building I'd assumed was a garage. Now that I looked at it more closely I saw it was a tiny cottage. He paid no attention to me, but clumped across the cement pavement in his heavy, ankle-high workman's boots. He wore red swim trunks and carried a rolled-up towel, which he flipped open and spread on a sunny spot of ground. Then he lay down on his back and closed his eyes. His skin was tanned a deep, even, mahogany brown, and his smooth, hairless chest gleamed with oil.

I said, "Hi."

He raised his head and looked in my direction. "Oh, hi. Visiting Jane?" His long, sun-streaked blond hair spilled onto the towel as he lay back down.

"No, Wanda."

"Ah, Wanda." His eyes closed again. He stretched, flexed muscular arms, and went limp.

"I'm Dorothy."

"How do." He sounded sleepy. "Rafe."

When I emerged from the water some time later I tiptoed around him and closed the porch door carefully so that it wouldn't slam.

The evenings were lively, filled with conversation and card-playing. Cap'n Jane had an endless supply of jokes and told them well, making everyone laugh except Bradleigh, who just looked confused. Suppers were a communal affair I was welcome to join, and yellow snapper was always on the menu. Cap'n Jane and I cooked while Wanda took a little rest in her room and Bradleigh sat on the screened porch mending fishing rods. Rafe, who was a serious vegetarian, would appear wearing a shirt unbuttoned to the waist and carrying a pot of something macrobiotic, which we could share if we wished although he never ate any of our food. His face, when I saw it up close, looked older than his body.

Rafe had just received a long letter from his fiancée in London, and he sat down at the table to read it aloud. When he came to parts like, "When I'm alone with you I'm going to—" he would say, "I'll just skip this bit." He made sure to read us the lead-ins, though. Rafe's fiancée was coming to Key West in two weeks to marry him. She seemed to be under the impression that he was a realtor, although in fact he did odd jobs around the marina and wrote poetry, trying to break into the greeting card market.

Wanda came up behind him, leaning her hands on the table, one on each side of him, peering over his shoulder at the letter. She rested her white head against his blond one, and without looking up, he gave her hand a couple of pats that seemed meant to be consoling.

Later, when Wanda and I were alone, she said, "Rafe and I are lovers."

"I was wondering how old he is."

"How old do you think he is?"

"I don't know. Twenty-nine? Thirty?"

"He'd be thrilled." Her voice hardened. "He's my age."

"But what about the fiancée?"

"They love each other very much." She said it solemnly, like a child repeating a lesson.

"But don't you mind?"

"Oh, it's okay. I mean, he told me right away. I can handle it." She looked at me. "I guess I can handle it, or am I kidding myself?"

She managed to get a day off and we visited the Museum of the Atocha, a Spanish galleon that had capsized in a storm while carrying a load of gold bullion and emeralds. After years of searching, a man named Mel Fisher had found the sunken treasure on a reef somewhere off the Keys. I'd seen a documentary about him on TV a few years earlier and had recognized the name when Wanda mentioned it to me once as we'd been weeding my Vermont garden. Brushing away a cloud of blackflies, she'd confided that she'd hatched a scheme to solve her money problems once and for all. If she joined one of Mel Fisher's treasure-hunting expeditions as a member of the crew, she'd be entitled to a share of any profits. "I'd be willing to do anything!" she'd said. I'd seldom seen her so excited. "Just one gold bar!" she'd cried. "Oh god, just one emerald! That's what I really want, an emerald! It would be soooo great!" Fervently she'd clasped her hands around the rake handle. "I know what you're thinking. You think I don't really mean it. But you're wrong. I wrote Mel Fisher a letter." With a big grin, she waited for my reaction.

"You did?"

"Yup. Offered to be ship's cook. It so happens I know some people who know him."

"Well! Sounds exciting." I didn't want to burst her bubble, though I thought she was too old to stand a chance. If she were a college student, maybe.

Actually, it was surprisingly easy to imagine her as a deckhand, or a cook sweating in a ship's galley. She owned a white buccaneer shirt with long sleeves cut very full, which she wore with her best jeans whenever she needed to dress up. In this outfit she looked rather dashing.

When I got to Key West I discovered that the idea wasn't as fantastic as it had sounded in Vermont. She did know people who'd invested in Fisher's previous voyages, or gone along as members of his crew. In the bar at the marina she introduced me to a few. One man had bought a house with his share of the treasure. A woman who'd had a smaller share was supplementing her Social Security by selling a silver coin every now and then.

Wanda's application had been turned down, yet she hadn't given up hope and was still trying to pull strings. But age was overtaking Mel Fisher, and the expeditions he was planning were stalled by a lawsuit with the State of Florida, which wanted a share of his treasure.

On my second night in Key West, Cap'n Jane and Bradleigh took me to the bar where they'd met and I got to hear their story again, this time from Jane.

"He just stayed on," she said, giving her deep, rasping laugh. "Isn't that right, Bradleigh?"

"That's right." He was drinking steadily and she was matching him, shot for shot, while I drank club soda.

She laughed again. "Is that sweet, or what?"

Jane and I got into a heavy discussion about psychoanalysis, about which she'd done a lot of reading, and then Wanda showed up from work. That was when she introduced me to the people who knew Mel Fisher.

Cap'n Jane and Bradleigh went to the bar most evenings, but they didn't take me again because I didn't drink. They didn't hold it against me though. In fact Jane took a liking to me. It was impossible to tell what Bradleigh thought.

Jane offered to take me out fishing in the boat. "For free," she explained, so I wouldn't think she was trying to drum up business. "The first day I don't have a paying customer we'll go, if you don't mind short notice."

I didn't, of course, since I had plenty of time on my hands, and I was pleased to be asked, especially since I'd never fished in my life except for catching minnows in a bathing cap when I was a child. "I'd love it," I said. "Thanks a lot."

Throwing an arm across my shoulder, Jane said to Wanda, "She can stay as long as she wants."

The fishing trip took place two days before I was to leave and lasted all day, which felt a bit long to me, though not to Cap'n Jane and Bradleigh. Jane tied a big straw hat to my head with a string so the wind wouldn't blow it off, and then she started the engine and roared out to sea, steering the boat expertly between the buoys as the waves slapped us up and down and the brim of my hat flapped madly. We visited several reefs, where Bradleigh tried patiently to teach me how to fish. After many attempts I managed to haul a couple of undersize yellow snapper into the boat before the pelicans riding the waves nearby could steal them from my line.

Cap'n Jane caught half a dozen sizable fish in the course of the day. But it was Bradleigh who was truly amazing. He was like a highly-specialized machine with built-in radar, the aim of a guided missile, and a deep grasp of fish psychology. It was moving to watch him, like seeing a great actor perform. He would lazily, almost indifferently, let the line run out and then suddenly, powerfully, and for no reason I could discern begin to reel it in, with a fish struggling at the end of it. I felt like applauding. As the ice chest filled I tried to get him to tell me his secret, but all he could say was, "You sorta get a feel for it."

On my last day Wanda had to work as usual, so I visited the old, walled cemetery and then drove to a plant nursery I'd looked up in the Yellow Pages. I wanted to express my appreciation by planting something in the back yard.

I wandered around the nursery for a while with a cart, picking out impatiens. They seemed to grow differently in the tropics, thick and bushy, and the colors became more vivid and jewel-like, piercing and sensual, especially at twilight. In Vermont they looked—I don't know, crisper. Maybe it was the fine veil of moisture suspended in the air of the Keys, or the light reflected in strange ways off the warm gulf waters, or something unique to the raffish little island itself. I filled my cart with pink impatiens, and coral and purple and orange and magenta—Matisse colors that seemed to clash, unlikely couplings that would melt together gorgeously as the sun went down.

When I got back to the house I started planting right away. The soil seemed very poor, hard, and filled with grit and whitish-gray stones—coral, most likely—that couldn't have been more different from the loose, dark humus of my Vermont garden, where years of careful cultivation had deepened and enriched the soil. As I struggled to jam the little plants into the ground, I felt more and more pessimistic about their future. I gave each one a cupful of water—there was no hose—and went into the house thinking, "If they grow it'll be a miracle."

The next day I headed north and my winter life—my suburban life—swallowed me up as soon as I got home, the way it always does. Once in a while when I was on the point of falling asleep the memory of Wanda and my week in Key West would flash across my awareness, vivid and disturbing.

In April Wanda sent me a letter to say she would be leaving for Vermont in a couple of weeks and to ask when I was coming up. She was looking forward to getting her hands in the dirt. She was sure this was the year the clematis would really take off. She'd been thinking that if we planted a lot of daffodils out in the meadow, next spring they would be spectacular.

She didn't know, nor did I, that the summer would prove to be her last. Late in the fall the tumor that had been pressing on her spine would declare itself with a blast of such pain that even Wanda the Strong had to be rushed to the emergency room. By midwinter, she would be dead.

At the end of her letter she wrote:

> I never told you I was positive those impatiens you planted wouldn't grow. Especially since for sure I wasn't going to mess with them. But I was wrong, they grew anyway, and they were absolutely incredible (still are)! Fabulous! Jane says you can come back and be our gardener any time.
>
> Love always,
> Wanda

Bones of the Earth

On a back road in Vermont, a small house sits atop a retaining wall made of enormous, rough-cut granite blocks. The mighty wall seems to have been there forever, but in fact it was built only a dozen years ago. The stones came from an old barn foundation some distance up the road. The barn burned down many years ago—a common fate of wooden structures in this land of woodstoves and long winters—but the foundation stones remained, half buried in the earth, and concealed by the brambles that grew up to fill the cellar hole.

The stones were not forgotten, however. Such stones are valued in Vermont, and not just because they are worth money—more and more as the years go by and these old monoliths become scarcer. Vermonters are frugal folk who know the value of a dollar, but I doubt that money was uppermost in the minds of the men I've seen, shaking their heads as they wondered aloud how their ancestors managed to cut and transport such giants. Actually, the methods used are known, so the wonderment is really at the skill of these long-dead men, and the enormous amount of work they seem to have taken in their stride.

And there is a wonderment at the stones themselves, as if they possessed mythic qualities like those attributed to certain fabled jewels—the Star of India, say. I've seen men in beat-up jeans and muddy boots fall into a reverie in front of stones, clutching their chins and gently nodding their heads for what seemed a long time.

The retaining wall was built to create a terrace where chairs could be placed overlooking the view, and plants could be grown. Now a cottage garden of herbs and old-fashioned perennials fills most of the space between the wall and the house, which used to be a one-room schoolhouse.

In this garden, stone is everywhere and thyme is inescapable. Thyme creeps along the seams of the terrace of lovingly-fitted slate, forming great mats on which the visitor unavoidably treads and the two resident cats love to roll. The crushed thyme fills the air with a spicy fragrance that, like all fragrances, is hard to describe: bracing, not at all sweet, and yet so pleasurable that as you draw in your breath the thought comes to mind, "Ah—life should always be exactly the way it is this moment."

The wall, the garden, the old schoolhouse, and the owners, a long-married couple named Blythe and Evans Clinchy, seem to be welded together into a unit, so that it is hard to imagine one of them without the others.

Of course the old cemetery that presses up against the side of the house is part of the picture, too. You notice the cemetery when you come to visit and then it slips out of mind, perhaps because it is set a little lower than the house and because the terrace faces the other way. But it is always there.

Also, in a sense, there is Alex Jurkiewicz, the moody, silent mason who raised the wall, built the steps, and fitted together the slabs that form the terrace floor. Although he is seldom to be seen about the Clinchy place these days, his spirit has seeped into it. Sooner or later his name has a way of coming up.

"We're terrace builders, you know," Evans Clinchy remarked to me one mellow September afternoon. "We're wall builders. We'd built two before we bought this place." I had arrived half an hour before, and Evans, a craggy-faced, very tall man nearing seventy, had as usual grabbed me in a hug that mashed my nose against the middle of his chest. He was wearing a couple of faded, much-laundered sweatshirts, wrinkled pants, and muddy sneakers. One of his large collection of baseball caps was thrust well down over shaggy gray hair that stuck out on the sides. The visor shaded eyes in which an ironical twinkle lurked. Evans doesn't look much like the distinguished educator he is—educational guru, some would say—especially on hot days when he wears the cap with the small, battery-operated fan on top that is supposed to cool his head. He wasn't wearing it today, for there was an autumnal bite in the air and frost was in the offing. He and Blythe were putting the garden to bed.

"It's such a mess," said Blythe, her tone apologetic. "There's nothing to see." We were passing a waist-high clump of purple asters covered with butterflies, orange-and-black monarchs that had stopped to refuel on their migration south. They were sipping nectar with such absorption that our presence didn't trouble them. "I did nothing in the garden all summer," she said. "I had these awful deadlines. And now the summer's over! I can't stand it!"

"She's been under a lot of pressure," Evans growled. He hates it when Blythe feels tense.

"And he just keeps turning out books!"

This was true, but I tended to lose sight of the fact because Evans seldom brings it up. Turning out books is something he takes for granted. He has been writing for a living for fifty years, ever since his days on the *Hartford Times,* where he doubled as police reporter during the day and drama critic at night. Blythe, on the other hand, came late to scholarship, while raising three children. Evans pushed her to use her mind, she says. Blythe is one of those feminists who are cemented into long, mutually rewarding relationships with men who complement them as perfectly as can be expected in an imperfect world.

I looked around. It was true that the garden, crowded and floppy by design, was at the moment floppier than usual. The spent perennials needed cutting back. A late white phlox, planted by Blythe in memory of her mother-in-law, who loved phlox and grew it in her own garden, had gone mostly to seed and would be strewing the garden with magenta progeny soon, if steps weren't taken. I dipped my nose into a lingering cluster of blossoms, inhaling their sweetness. Like most of its neighbors, the phlox was growing in a sizable clump. You might say it needed dividing. Or you could simply call it stout and flourishing. "Garden seems fine to me," I said, and meant it. It had a lived-in look, like the comfortable, slightly shabby study of a scholar.

Fourteen years earlier, Blythe and Evans had first seen the old Dwinell schoolhouse that was now their summer home. The interior had been redone by an architect who had intended to live there and then changed his plans. He'd done a splendid job and the house was a jewel. On the other hand, it was too small for the Clinchys and had a few other drawbacks. But they'd bought it anyway. They'd had no choice, really, for fate had taken a hand. Blythe's grandparents had owned a summer house everyone called "The Schoolhouse." It was the place where she had spent her happiest hours as a child.

And there was the name—"Dwinell." She had heard it often when she was growing up, because her beloved grandfather had worked for years as a salesman for the Dwinell-Wright Coffee Company in Columbus, Ohio.

So when the realtor had shown her and Evans the old Dwinell schoolhouse, and mentioned that the small graveyard next door was the Dwinell cemetery and the farm up the road was the Dwinell farm, she'd known they'd found the place they were looking for.

"It was fated," she told me once, sounding a bit self-conscious since that's not the sort of thing Blythe says. "It was meant to be."

It seems right for Blythe and Evans to live in a school. Both are passionate educators, the kind whose passions stem from the antipathy they felt for the educations they had to put up with as children. Blythe, who is now a college professor and an expert on women's intellectual development, says she was totally lost in the big public schools she attended. Perhaps it was there that she learned to retreat into the silent, watchful, almost invisible presence she sometimes becomes in groups. But when Blythe feels at ease her dry wit emerges. She has the rare gift of giving you her utter and complete attention, and at such times her whole being seems to relax and open, with an effect that is seductive.

As for Evans, he describes his long career as an educational theorist and consultant as a "massive act of revenge" for having been excrutiatingly bored in school, which he considers "a form of child abuse no kid ought to be subjected to."

The main drawback to the Dwinell schoolhouse was that the yard was too small for a garden. Actually there was no yard, just a steep, fifteen-foot drop to a cow pasture. So after the Clinchys bought the house they also acquired the piece of land up the road where the old barn had once stood. They planned to use the foundation stones to build a retaining wall behind the house.

Evans likes to tell the story. "So we hired a garden consultant to lay out a terrace garden for us."

Blythe said, "Evans sketched a possible design. But our consultant told us a fifteen-foot wall was too high. And the garden we wanted was too big."

"It so happens that's exactly the garden we have now," Evans pointed out complacently.

"The consultant said, 'This can be a very fine garden if it's laid out correctly.'"

Evans gave a deep rumble of laughter. "So we fired him." The thatch of gray hair that stuck out below his cap flew up as he threw back his head. Firing the consultant, I could see, had given him much pleasure.

Blythe cried, "There is so much in my life that has to be done correctly! Bibliographies, footnotes. . . . When it came to the garden, I really didn't want any standards. I had a vision of a cottage garden, like the ones I'd loved in Cornwall, all higgledy-piggledy. I like plants that crawl and flop around. I never liked formal French gardens. I'm not good at preplanning. It's trial and error—I'm always rethinking the garden. And I read garden books, of course."

I asked if Evans was the planner. I was curious to know how the Clinchys collaborated. Was she the general and he the foot soldier? Earlier I'd heard her saying, "Burgee"—her nickname for him—"I have many projects for you. The goldenrod is invading. The Virginia creeper is taking over. . . ."

Evans said, "Neither of us really plans. Alex did it all. He'd never done anything this big. The artistry!"

They both fell silent, contemplating Alex. Blythe said, as she always does, "Alex is a genius."

Stone men—that's how I think of them, for the word "mason" brings to mind bricks laid up, end to end, with machinelike regularity—seem to be unlike other construction workers, or garden workers either. I've known several fairly well, and all have something strange about them. They are artists, really. Visionaries with an eye always scanning the landscape, judging what seem to be piles of rubbish or mere protrusions in the earth, estimating the size of stones the rest of us may not even have noticed and calculating the cost in time and labor to extract them from the earth and transport them someplace else. Stone men, at least the ones I've known, seem to find it agonizingly difficult to put a price on their work.

I first saw Alex at the Clinchys' place, which wasn't surprising because he practically lived there for a year. It was after he'd finished the wall, so I never got a chance to see how he worked with the backhoe operator whose task it had been to trundle each of the granite monoliths down the road from the old barn foundation and then fit it into place according to Alex's directions—a job requiring much judgment and skill on the part of both men.

When I did meet Alex he was down on his knees, his wiry back bent, his face close to the ground as he tenderly fitted stones together to make a path to the Clinchys' front door. Lank dark hair hung down, screening his face. He tossed it back when Blythe introduced us, muttering something I couldn't hear, and his eyes as they flicked over me were dark, wary, and wild. He wasn't ruddy, as most outdoor workers are. Instead he had the grayish pallor of a coal miner.

I saw him at the Clinchys' several times after that, but we didn't exchange any more words until several years later when he did a small job for me, and I was never quite sure whether he recognized me. He was always absorbed in his work, shoveling sand and tamping it into place, reaching into a pile of stones to find the one that would fit, or crawling along the ground eyeballing a step he was building.

Stones have been called "the bones of the earth," and in many a garden they provide the skeleton, to be fleshed out by the plants we Westerners are apt to think of first when we hear the word "garden." Plants and stones complement and balance each other; both are essential. Of course in Chinese and Japanese gardens stones are considered as important as plants, or even more so. Whole gardens may consist of nothing but stones, which are used to symbolize mountains, streams, and other elements of the landscape. These stones are acknowledged to possess spiritual qualities that serve to link even the smallest garden to the vast earth itself—even to the cosmos.

In American gardens, stone tends to be more utilitarian, but it never quite loses its ancient power to put us in touch with levels of meaning that go deeper than our transient enjoyment of color and fragrance. A primitive resonance always remains latent in stone. Or perhaps what remains latent is our own "Stonehenge impulse," our tendency to respond to stone with awe, as if it possessed a quality that goes beyond the obvious, physical qualities of hardness, strength, and durability: a kind of spiritual force.

There is a certain stone I see whenever I drive along a dirt road a few miles from the Clinchys' place. The stone, which is about the size of a one-room house, appears huge, not only because it stands isolated in a grassy field that slopes gently downhill from the road, but because there is nothing behind the stone but sky—no trees, no brush, nothing but the shifting panorama of the clouds.

The shape of this stone is curious. Instead of being rounded, like most boulders left behind by ancient glaciers, it is faceted. It definitely has the look of having been moved to its present position. By whom? I can't imagine. It seems too large to have been dug up by a farmer or even by one of the local road construction crews; there are no other stones lying on the ground nearby.

I always admire the stately way it sits, facing outward toward the valley and the hills beyond, as if presiding over its domain and assuring that all remains well there. I can almost see human figures capering around it in an ancient, ceremonial dance. Once that picture has sprung into my mind I always wonder how long the stone has stood there and feel an urge to approach it on foot and worship it—whatever that might mean.

Then, too, there are certain huge stones that grow in the yards of ordinary houses. I can think of two that I know. These stones, like the tips of stone icebergs, are obviously outcroppings of much larger, underground masses. I don't happen to know any of the people who live in these houses, and I'm curious about how "their" stones affect them. I've put quotes around "their" because the stones have been in place so much longer than the people, and will so obviously outlast them, that it seems ridiculous to think in terms of ownership; unless the people belong to the stones.

I'm referring now to stones so big they dwarf their people and rival the size of the houses. A stone such as this has too much presence to ignore. It defines your space. It *is* your garden. One of the householders has tried to tame the stone in his yard by planting a few flowers around the base of it—a handful of tulips, a line of gladioli, a rosebush on a fan-shaped trellis—but the effect is like that of a lace ruffle on an elephant.

I suppose it might be possible to make a magnificent hanging rock garden of such a stone, but it would be a life's work. You'd have to do your gardening from a ladder. And the lace ruffle problem would always be lying in wait for you.

About the question of worship, I remember visiting San Francisco some years ago, when the management of Golden Gate park was facing an unexpected problem. There are some fine Asian gardens in the park, thanks to the generosity of the city's large Asian population, and these receive many visitors. On some occasion or other, a traffic control stanchion had been placed in one of the gardens and forgotten. It was a waist-high piece of stone of a phallic shape, rather handsome, really, but identical to hundreds of others used by the city's department of public works.

But in this garden there was only one, which made it stand out more than if there had been fifteen or twenty. By the time I saw it had grown mossy and looked quite venerable. A short time before, it had happened to come to the attention of the park maintenance people, who wanted to remove it. This created a tremendous furor that got into the newspapers. The trouble was, a number of people had begun to worship the stone. They left small offerings at its base and held religious ceremonies there at dawn. The worshippers wanted the stone left exactly where it was, and the fact that it was a traffic stanchion—this was explained to them—didn't seem to make any difference. Possibly the "stone" was even made of concrete.

I left the city before the problem was resolved, so I don't know how it came out.

What are we to make of this?

We could roll our eyes and say, "Oh well, California . . ."

We could sigh—or laugh—over the gullibility of mankind, or fume about the foolishness of religion and superstition, and how little difference there is between them, really.

We could shrug, say something about "ethnicities," and turn the whole matter over to the Human Relations Board and let them worry about it.

But I think this is simply a case of the Stonehenge impulse popping up unexpectedly.

Certain people are more prone to the impulse than others, and although it's partly a learned—often a cultural—response, it also seems to be partly innate.

I know a particularly gifted stone man who believes that stones contain spirits that talk to him and even call to him from a distance to come and dig them up, although they may lie half-buried in fields where he's never been. He thinks the voices he hears have something to do with aliens. This man has been in communication with stones since childhood, and the other kids teased him about it so much that he's learned not to mention it except to people he trusts. "It's a hard path," he said once, with tears in his eyes.

This man is at the extreme end of the Stonehenge-impulse continuum, but plenty of people are sensitive to stone to a greater or lesser degree. And if a few of them happen to focus their attention on a particular stone—even a former traffic stanchion—admiring and then revering it, before you know it something very like the Old Religion may start to crystallize around it.

This Old Religion, which newer religions have often gone to great lengths to stamp out while at the same time appropriating many of its symbols, is nature worship. Trees, animals, water, the sun—all have been used as conduits through which human beings express their reverence for the source of life itself. Often fertility rites of one sort or another become part of this religion. Perhaps the shape of the traffic stanchion may have stirred up this association.

But why revere stones? Though certainly part of nature, they appear at first and even second glance to be quite dead. What have these hard, inert lumps of matter to do with procreation, with the sources of life? There have been stories in the press lately about the discovery of what may be primitive life forms, or their precursors, in meteorites that have fallen to earth. I've even read theories by reputable scientists that life on earth may have come about in this very way—by the salting of earth's surface, over eons of time, by life-bearing stones from outer space. If this proves to be true, my stone-loving friend's theory that there are aliens in certain stones may not be as fantastic as it seems. Even if the "aliens" aren't little green men with big heads (not that

he's ever said they were), maybe stones bear traces or re-
minders of something like life out there in the cosmos
that might, just might, be connected with the life we
know here on earth.

I sat on the terrace drinking red wine with the Clinchys.
Our faces were turned eastward, toward the valley and
the hills beyond. It was late in the afternoon. Below us,
at the foot of the wall, a herd of brown-and-white cows
ambled along in single file, heading home to the barn.
The lead cow wore a bell around her neck that tinkled
every time she took a step, filling the valley with music.
The landscape was a deep, juicy green, except for a few
trees that had begun to turn scarlet. In a matter of
weeks, a blaze of red and gold would cover the hills.

Blythe said, "We love to sit here in the evening. The
light is just extraordinary."

We sat drinking, saying nothing for a while. Slowly,
the sun sank behind the cemetery at our backs as an
amber glow spread over the valley.

A cold wind stirred, and Blythe drew her sweater
closer. "I hate to see the end of all this," she said, glanc-
ing around the garden. "I meant to do so much more. I
never got around to dividing the hostas. The poor things
are terribly crowded."

Evans leaned forward. "I object to her denigrating the
garden." He refilled our glasses. "Her dreams are greater
than anyone could carry out."

Blythe said, "We might donate a little plot of our land
to the cemetery."

"It's full," Evans explained.

"Then we could be buried there. It doesn't feel ghoul-ish. It feels right."

The light was failing fast now, blurring the edges of the garden. Everywhere I looked, plant met stone—clung to it, leaned on it, draped over it—as closely joined as the man and woman who sat beside me sipping their wine. The amber glow faded to gray. Thyme crept into the cracks in the terrace floor, silently and imperceptibly crumbling the stone into dust.

The Woods

The Eastern white pine, known in England as the Weymouth pine, is the tallest conifer of the northeastern United States. It is often described in books as "magnificent" and "stately." The trunks grow so long and straight that they were prized for the masts of sailing vessels. Yet these mighty trees are vulnerable: to a weevil that likes to tunnel in their terminal shoots; to blister rust, which causes cankers on the branches and is carried by currants and gooseberries, which must be removed for a distance of 900 feet in areas where the disease is endemic; and, since their loftiness makes them prey to winds, to blowdown.

The greatest threat to the white pine, of course, is man. Although the trees are capable of growing to a hundred and fifty feet, nowadays a hundred is rare. Few woodlot owners care to wait a century for the trees to reach their full maturity before trucking them off to the sawmill.

✦

The woods behind our Vermont house consisted of nineteen acres of white pines. They covered the hill and came down to the edge of the clearing. Every morning when I stepped outside on the porch, they were the first thing I saw. Sometimes when I raised my eyes to the ridge, behind which the first glow of sunrise was beginning to appear, a line from the Psalms would come into my head: "I will lift up mine eyes unto the hills, from whence cometh my help." The words felt deeply true, although it was hard to say exactly how I was being helped, except by a feeling that I was a part of something greater than myself and was, at that moment, perfectly in tune with it.

The stand of white pines behind the house was locally rather famous. The trees had been planted in 1907 by a man whose name is unknown to me but who was clearly of some vision. The trees had been prized, pruned, and selectively culled for decades, so that as they grew there was always sufficient space between them. Now nearing the century mark, each tree had become a giant.

The care the trees had received over the years had made the woods cathedral-like. Shafts of light slanted down as if from clerestory windows, picking out the ferns that reveled in the dampness, and the mica-flecked boulders that reared up through the blanket of fallen needles. In the dim silence the smooth, well-spaced trunks receded into the distance like gothic columns in a sanctuary. In this realm of verticality the eye was drawn upward and the back instinctively straightened.

At the time we bought our house, the realtor had pointed out rather casually that the woods were not included in the property. But we were not to worry. They belonged to a local landowner who was fond of looking at them whenever he drove down our road. He was immensely wealthy, the realtor assured us, and could afford to indulge himself in such pleasures. He would never cut them down.

So we didn't worry. We took the woods for granted. Except for the dirt road, they were all we could see from our house. We assumed they would always be there, untouched and unchanged.

But the realtor's "never" turned out to be only six years. The tax laws changed, and as a result the owner decided to sell. He sent an emissary to ask if we wanted to buy the pinewoods. If not, he planned to cut the trees for timber.

Cut the trees! We were thunderstruck. How could this be? We knew the owner had a perfect right—after all, he was in the lumbering business, and had bought his thousands of acres in order to cut the trees and sell them, presumably—but not these woods, surely not these! Why, he loved them! The realtor had said so.

But as soon as we imagined how it would be to look out the windows at acres and acres of stumps, it became clear to us that we were really the ones who loved the woods. They had become essential to us—as the owner had no doubt guessed. So although we could ill afford to buy more land, we scraped together the money and bought it anyway.

Once the pines were ours, I began to feel a responsibility for them. I acquired a few books with titles like

Woodlot Management that explained how to "assess their potential" and bring about "timber stand enhancement" and "wildlife habitat improvement." I found the books instructive—in Vermont I was always learning something new—and I came to feel that my liberal suburban belief that it was bad to cut down a tree, any tree, was too limited. Trees had their uses, which my Vermont neighbors seemed to understand and rely on. They thinned their woods to improve them, cut firewood selectively, tapped the maple trees for syrup, and did a certain amount of logging; yet the state remained densely wooded.

Vermonters are not sentimental about their trees, although they care about them deeply. They know that trees spring up easily in New England, and only regular mowing or grazing keeps them from taking over every field. Much Yankee energy has been spent over the centuries in cutting down trees to clear the land for farming. Since wood is the universal building material and everyone has at least one wood stove, more trees are always being cut for firewood and to feed the small, local sawmills that are still fairly common.

In the last century, virtually all of Vermont's forests were decimated to feed a voracious, East Coast lumber industry. This is hard to imagine, because nowadays Vermont is so heavily forested. But the present woods are not old-growth stands; virtually none of those remain. Today, due to economic forces, heavy lumbering has moved out to the West Coast and up to Canada, and many family farms are being abandoned. As a result, Vermont's woodlands are expanding rapidly.

We didn't do much with our woods except hunt for mushrooms after a rain, note where the wild orchids grew, collect pine needles to mulch my blueberries, or dig up an occasional barrowful of leaf mould to nourish the delphiniums. Mostly we just looked at them. Such mild activities seemed to fall into the category of "Recreation and Aesthetics," to which one of my books devoted a page, stating, in a way I found reassuring, that this was "of most importance to many landowners." In other words, it was all right to do nothing with our woods.

One August day, when we had owned the woods for five years, we decided to take a drive to Montreal and sample some of the urban pleasures we occasionally found ourselves missing. The sky looked threatening as we set off. A thick layer of greenish clouds pressed low over the hills and churned in a way that made me feel uneasy.

By the time we returned it was after midnight. As we neared home we drove through intermittent rain and patches of dense fog. For the last twenty minutes of the trip, ours was the only car on the road. The countryside seemed darker than usual, and there were no lights in the villages, as if the power were out.

Finally, we turned into our road. It was obvious that rain had fallen heavily during our absence. We could hear Jug Brook roaring in the ravine, and water was streaming down the ditches on the sides of the road. Leaves and fallen branches lay everywhere. A dense mist beaded like rain on our windshield.

As the road climbed upward, Joe drove slowly to avoid the branches on the road. Eventually we reached the house. It was completely dark although I'd left an outside light on. We pulled into the driveway and saw that our cleaning lady's station wagon was parked near the kitchen door. We exchanged puzzled glances. Beryl was supposed to have been there in our absence, but she should have left hours ago.

We got out of the car. The fog pressed around us as we took the flashlight from the glove compartment and shone it into the station wagon. It was empty and looked normal.

We let ourselves into the house and found that the power was out. Otherwise, everything seemed to be as we had left it. Beryl was gone, but she had left us a note on the kitchen table.

> As you can see we had some big storm! Lost power after 5:30 about the time storm hit couldn't vacuum so changed your bed and did rest of house work. Went down in cellar for a while, I thought maybe the roof would come off but it didn't. People got here about 7:30 to start cutting trees out of road. Lots of trees were blown down as you can see. Don't know when they will have the big tree out of the road, can't get through so am walking out. Men are out there with chain saws had to cut trees all the way up here out of the road there is more up the road. Call me and good luck with the mess. I will get car tomorrow morning sometime.

Good luck with the mess! What mess?

We pulled our coats back on and went outside. But the fog had grown even denser, and bounced the light from our flashlights back at us so that we could see nothing. Rain started falling again. After a while we gave up and went in the house.

We slept fitfully. Early the next morning we threw on raincoats and went outside. The fog had not yet lifted, and curtains of drenching, opaque mist shifted and blew. Between them we caught glimpses of the damage the storm had done.

Four ancient sugar maples with gnarled and massive trunks had been growing in a line, shielding the house from the road. They were as much a part of the spirit of the place as the house itself. Now two of them were gone, wrenched off their stumps. Later we would count the rings and find that the trees had been almost two hundred years old. The third sugar maple had been splintered so savagely that it looked as if we would lose it, too. The fourth was still standing, although half its crown dangled precariously, creaking whenever the wind blew.

It was the sugar maples that had blocked the road. We could see their enormous limbs lying where the emergency crew had dragged them aside, leaving just enough room for a car to pass.

We wandered around the clearing, picking our way between the branches that had been strewn on the ground. We came to the pond. Two spruce trees had toppled in headfirst, and a big pine lay stretched from bank to bank like a bristly bridge. Behind the pond a narrow band of trees remained standing—by some miracle the storm had spared them—but beyond lay utter chaos. The white pines on the hill had been devastated. Most had been toppled with such force that they lay on the ground, their enormous root systems ripped out of the ground and exposed. Others had been twisted on their stumps by the wind, the way a cook twists a handful of spaghetti. The woods we thought we had saved were gone.

We couldn't take it in. Nineteen acres of woods had vanished in a day.

A semblance of woods was still there, but the appearance was deceptive. Most of the pines that seemed to be standing had actually been shredded at the base and were leaning against each other for support. They swayed and groaned, threatening to crash to the ground at any moment. Loggers call such trees widowmakers— and they were everywhere. We peered into the wreckage through the fringe of trees that had been spared, but didn't dare get any closer.

We told each other that the house was safe and no one had been hurt—that was what was important. Standing hand in hand like orphaned children we said all the things you say when disaster hits. My God, I can't believe it. This is incredible. Oh my God, look at that.

Things would have to be done, that much was obvious. But we had no idea where or how to begin. How did you get an eighty-foot tree out of a pond—let alone three trees? We started picking up branches from the lawn and then stood with them in our hands, wondering where to put them. We were in shock—two soft, city people confronted with an event that was completely outside our experience.

After a while we started hearing chainsaws. The town road crew was working its way up the road in our direction. The phone began ringing with calls from neighbors: "Heard you were hit bad. What was it, a tornado?" Beryl arrived to pick up her station wagon, bringing news and a thermos of coffee for which we were grateful, as the power was still out and our stove was electric.

People were saying it had been a tornado, she said, although nobody had seen a funnel. We weren't the only ones who'd been hit. The storm had followed a narrow path, touching down here and there in a straight line for several miles. Big tracts of woods had been skipped completely. A roof had blown off somebody's garage, she'd heard. But the properties of our neighbors on both sides were fine. Untouched, she said. Their woods had hardly lost a tree. Weird, really.

The sound of chainsaws kept growing louder. A couple of times we heard a huge, reverberating crash; a widowmaker had fallen to the ground. Around noon the road crew reached us.

Vermont has thousands of miles of dirt roads where many Vermonters live, and the local road crews serve a vital function. They are constantly spreading gravel, mending ditches, repairing washouts, and cutting back the trees that keep encroaching on the roadway. Today the regular crew had been amplified by others. I recognized the clerk at the hardware store and a dairy farmer who lived nearby, and there were a couple of men I didn't know. They'd been handling chainsaws all their lives—neither Joe nor I had ever even touched one—and in their hands the screaming machines sliced through the fallen limbs of the sugar maples, whipping off the smaller branches and cutting the thicker sections into short lengths that were tossed aside. I asked if they could take down the maple that had been badly splintered, but they said they couldn't. The remaining limbs would have to be cut away first, and they weren't supposed to do any climbing. Same thing for the maple with the dangling section of crown. I would have to find a tree man to deal with them.

One of the road crew asked if I wanted him to come back and cart the wood away, and I said, "Sure," thankful to have one less thing to deal with. Only later I recalled that he had a firewood business on the side. At the time I was still too stunned to think about my woodstoves or realize that the fallen maples would have yielded enough summer firewood to last me the rest of my life.

The whine of the chainsaws, a sound we would hear every day for the rest of the summer, receded up the road. In the woods another widowmaker fell to the ground with a tremendous crash.

Across the road, beyond the power company's right-of-way, a neighbor's trees climbed to the ridge, untouched. The storm had passed them by. "Why us?" I kept thinking.

Joe went in the house. He'd had enough for one day, and he knows how to shut down when he's reached his limit.

I don't. I have to take it all in. I crossed the road and made my way down to the stream, heading for the chair under the big spruce.

But there was no chair. No spruce. The storm had blown down the spruce and it lay prone across the field, clutching beneath its branches a grove of young birch and maple that had gone down with it. The chair must be somewhere under the pile.

The waterfall was thundering and the stream was running high and wild. The torrent boiled down the channel, clawing at the roots of the trees along the bank, most of which were still standing. If the water kept racing along at this rate, it would undermine the roots and some of these trees would fall as well.

I stood for a while staring into the stream. The usually crystalline water was opaque, and looked cold and unfriendly. I turned away and gazed back at the house. Now that the row of ancient sugar maples had been torn away, the place seemed exposed and vulnerable.

Behind the house rose the hill and the wreckage of the woods. Only yesterday, the pines had crowned the ridge. I had known their profiles intimately. Now they were gone and the naked line of the ridge was alien and disorienting. I might have been looking at any hill, anywhere.

I thought of the nights when I had sat on the porch as if in a darkened theater waiting for the curtain to rise. After a while, the moon would appear from behind the ridge, bright as a searchlight when full. I would wait for it to clear the tip of the tallest pine. I had loved to see the moon riding the sky above that particular tree, but I would not see it again. Today that tree lay stretched across the pond.

I stood in the field and cried.

When I got back to the house, a rusted-out pickup truck was parked at the foot of the driveway with a man and a boy standing next to it. The man, shaggy-haired and wild-eyed, looked like one of the aging hippies who still live in the Vermont woods. His face had the broken capillaries and spongy nose of a drinker.

The boy, who seemed to be about fifteen, had big hands and feet that stuck out of his too-short sleeves and pants legs as if he'd had a recent growth spurt. He asked me, "Is there any work you need done?"

I had nothing but work to be done—that was plain to see. I said, "What kind can you do?"

"Anything you want!" he cried. "Clean up! Anything with wood, you name it." The boy had a handsome face with a well-developed set of worry lines on his forehead.

"Well, we seem to have plenty of that."

He eyed the mounds of wood left behind by the road crew. "Do you need all that wood, could you maybe spare some?"

The man leaned toward me. "That was some storm, huh?" He gave me a grin that might once have been engaging. Now half his teeth were missing and his lips were chapped and crusted.

I said, "Tell you what, why don't you take what's on the far side of the road." Why should I give it all to the man with the firewood business? "And could you cut up the smaller limbs"—I showed him the size I wanted—"and pile them near the house for me?" They would be the perfect size for early-morning fires in my study, where I had a small Franklin stove.

"No problem!"

"You sure got hit," the man said. "Hey, you want me to go up that maple and cut that out for you?" He pointed to the dangling crown.

"Dad, it's too dangerous. We better get Charley."

"I did logging one time."

"We have a friend used to work for a tree surgeon," the boy said to me. "Only he's been out sick. He could come over tomorrow, maybe."

The boy seemed trustworthy, and I said, "That would be great." I'd been told I needed a tree man and had wondered where I would find one. Now perhaps one had found me. The boy promised to bring him the next day, and he and his father started pitching hunks of maple into their truck.

Tom Maclay, who advises me in all things connected with the land, dropped by that afternoon to say he'd heard about our trouble. As usual he was full of accurate information, which had come, this time, from "An Eye on the Sky," the Central Vermont weather report. Our storm had not been a tornado, he informed me. Tornadoes swirl, but this had been a so-called "straight-line wind," known in some parts of the world as a *derecho*. Such storms can spawn winds up to 100 miles an hour and virtually nonstop lightning. One had hit the Adirondacks a few years back and leveled literally millions of trees.

We walked around assessing the damage. What I needed was a logger, Tom said, and this might not cost as much as I thought. It might not cost anything, if I let the logger sell the timber for me. Stumpage was running in the neighborhood of $50 a thousand board-feet, and there must be—he did a quick mental calculation—at least 50,000 feet of downed timber in the woods. I might even make a few dollars, enough to pay for some of the additional cleanup. But I'd have to find the logger fast—in a matter of days—before rot started to set in. This would lower the value of the wood.

Tom's presence and his brisk, practical advice made me feel a little better. It always helps to be able to do something, and as long as I didn't have to drag those trees away myself, or spend money I could ill afford, I was glad to set to work. I could almost hear my mother's voice saying, "Stop moping and get busy," and the thought of her strengthened me.

As it happened, I knew a logger, or rather I knew of him. His name was Hank Benson, and when we first came to Vermont he and his wife and children had lived only a few houses up the road from us. I'd never met them, but I'd heard Hank Benson was a logger. He was said to be a good one, and more honest than most. It's easy for a logger to cheat the owner of the trees he cuts, by undercounting the number of board feet he delivers to the sawmill.

That night I gave him a call. He knew who I was right away—"You're the blue house? Got hit by the storm?"—and agreed to drop by the next day and look the situation over.

I awoke the next morning to the sound of chainsaws. The father and son who had come the day before were down in the road, sawing wood and piling it in their pickup truck. With them was the man who had worked for the tree surgeon. He'd been in an accident, he told me when I went outside. But now he was fine and would take down the maple if I wanted.

We walked over to the tree. He was a young man, still in his twenties, who had grown up in Canada. He was limping, but he shinned right up the tree with a pair of spikes fastened to his shoes and a stout rope looped around his body and between his legs. When he'd climbed high enough, he threw one end of the rope over a solid branch and let it dangle down where the father could pull it taut.

Slowly and carefully he dismembered the tree, limb by limb, lowering each of them to the ground with ropes. As the limbs reached the ground, the boy cut them up with his chainsaw. Meanwhile, his father kept pulling on the rope that bore the weight of the man in the tree, who kept climbing higher and higher. The day was sunny, with a bright blue sky—it was the first time the sun had shone since the storm—and the three seemed to be enjoying the job, bantering as they worked.

When the tree had come down, they moved over to the maple that still remained standing. The tree man climbed up and cut away the section of the crown that was dangling. What remained looked lopsided and ungainly, but he assured me that over time it would fill out.

They cut wood for the rest of the day, made me a neatly stacked woodpile, and left promising to return in a day or two to get the trees out of my pond. The tree man went home early, and I never saw him again. I later heard that he'd fallen out of a tree only a few weeks before and dislocated his hip. That was the reason he'd been limping. When I thought of him up in the tree, I winced. He must have been in pain, but he never complained.

Hank Benson dropped by around lunchtime. He turned out to be a tall, lanky man in tight blue jeans and a broad-brimmed Stetson hat with a feather and some sort of Indian amulet on the band. The brim shaded his bright blue eyes and his pierced ears had small silver earrings in them. He'd brought his son with him, a boy of about ten who never said a word. Hank told me they'd been walking around my place for an hour, looking things over. It would take him about six weeks to do the job, he said. The widowmakers didn't seem to faze him. But he would need a "stage," he said. This is a cleared, level piece of land, preferably near a road, where logs can be trimmed, cut into lengths, and stacked until the logging truck picks them up and takes them to the mill. Could he use the field on the far side of the driveway?

That would be fine, I said.

Later in the day he showed up again. This time he brought his skidder on a flatbed truck. The skidder is a large, noisy tractor designed for dragging logs out of the woods. He unloaded it and parked it in the "stage." Then he took off.

After that I didn't see much of him, except at a distance. He came every day, weather permitting, and usually brought his son. I would know he had arrived when I heard the rumbling of the skidder around eight in the morning.

The first task he tackled was to lay out a logging road on the hill. This would give him access to the woods and be used for dragging out the logs.

Once the road was cleared he spent most of his time in the woods, felling trees that hadn't fallen all the way to the ground, sawing off the larger limbs, and shifting the trunks around with the skidder. Sometimes I caught glimpses of the big red machine moving on the hill. Often it was hidden by brush, or behind a rise, and I could only hear it.

From time to time the sound of the skidder would grow steadily louder, and I would know Hank was dragging a load of logs down the logging road to the stage. Then I would go upstairs and stand by the window. From there I had a perfect view.

In a few minutes the skidder would emerge from the strip of woods the storm had spared. Hank would be sitting at the controls, high and handsome, with his young son on the seat beside him. Four or five huge logs dragged along the ground behind the machine, fanning out as the skidder rumbled into the middle of the stage.

Hank would dismount, and a ritual of fastening and unfastening chains began, the purpose of which was not always obvious. He trimmed the logs more closely and cut them to the right length. He nudged them here and dragged them there. He jumped in and out of the skidder, backing the machine or moving it forward.

He took great care of his chainsaw, and would stop work frequently to sit down on a log and oil it, or take it apart for sharpening. I'd seen a lot of men use chainsaws since I'd come to Vermont, but I'd never seen one who was so particular about caring for his tool. It must have been vital to his safety in the woods to be able to rely on it utterly. Or maybe it was something in the character of the man himself, a meticulousness, a pride in his craft.

Occasionally the boy slid over behind the controls of the skidder, and at his father's shouted directions carefully moved the big machine forward or backward. Or his father would let him do a little work with the chainsaw. I was amazed, because the child was so young. I wondered if Hank's father, too, had been a logger and had put Hank through the same sort of apprenticeship when he was a boy. No wonder Hank seemed to feel no fear, in an occupation that struck me as incredibly dangerous. A child has no real appreciation of risks, and driving the skidder must have felt like playing with the biggest toy in the world. I was witnessing the ancient and natural handing-on of knowledge and skills from father to son, in a way that is fast becoming obsolete in the modern world.

We got used to waking to the sound of chainsaws. The racket they made became a part of our lives for the rest of the summer. After a while we hardly noticed it. I actually found it soothing, for it meant that things were being done, necessary things. When the chainsaws fell silent I would wonder if something had gone wrong. Was someone hurt?

The loss of the trees continued to weigh heavily on our spirits. Yet the cleanup proceeded well. The hippie contingent winched the trees out of the pond, one by one, after the boy dived down under the water to secure the chains around the trunks. He wore flippers on his feet and a black rubber wetsuit, an outfit not often seen in Vermont, and he mentioned several times that he'd acquired it in California. "This boy won't be here long," I thought. And indeed he later became captain of a fishing boat off the coast of Oregon. I'm sure he did a fine job, having had plenty of experience with responsibility from taking care of his father.

Hank Benson worked day after day, dragging the trees out of the woods. I worried about his being injured by a falling tree, but he remained unhurt.

It amazed me that everything seemed to fall into place, as if some ecological process had been activated by the storm. In the natural world the death of anything— a mouse, a deer, a tree—immediately begins to attract insects such as flies, ants, and termites, as well as carrion eaters like hyenas, rats, and vultures. Bacteria multiply and fungi begin to grow, breaking down the dead organism into its component parts. Each creature provides something that another one needs for its survival. Were it not for these activities, the world would have been covered long ago by a dense layer of dead things unable to decompose.

The death of our woods had triggered a similar process, on a larger scale, only it involved people and machines as well as the silent processes of rot and decay. Even Joe and I had our parts to play, for as employers we channeled money into a chronically depressed local economy. As for myself, I was the coordinator of the project, the "general contractor."

One day I mentioned to Tom my astonishment at how soon after the storm the hippie father and his son had shown up to help, and how they'd even produced a tree man.

"Scavengers," he growled. He has little patience for hippies.

Well, maybe. They had needed firewood. But scavengers have their part to play in the scheme of things. And they'd been perfectly willing to work.

The cleanup was moving along steadily, but there was no denying that the once beautiful hill was now an unsightly mess. The operations of the logger left rawness behind: stumps like unhealed wounds and tons of sawn-off branches—"slash" in logging parlance—strewn on the ground. Tom and his grown sons hauled the slash into piles that towered higher than my head. They burned them on drizzly days, when there was less danger of a fire getting out of control.

No matter how much slash we burned, there was always more. I hired high school boys to collect the smaller pieces and worked with them to drag it away, tossing it over a rise into a small ravine that was out of sight of the house. There was no way to get rid of all of it. We had already spent more on the cleanup than we would make from selling the wood.

The once-green hill turned brown, and the brown began to fade to a deathly gray.

Tom said, "Don't worry. It'll grow back."

I was not comforted. It might grow back, but not in my lifetime.

He understood. "You'll be surprised what a change you see in five years—even four."

Tom was looking to the future, but it was too soon for me to do so. I still had mourning to do, and that takes time. It made no difference to me, not then, that the storm and its aftermath were only an episode in a long, long story, or that my connection with that particular hillside had been infinitesimal, a mere eye-blink, in comparison with the millennia it had existed. I took the whole thing personally.

One day, Hank Benson showed me a faint darkening at the base of one of the trunks and said that the trees had been nearing the end of their life span. Sure, he'd heard pines could live for hundreds of years—but these wouldn't have done so. Why not? Maybe pollution, maybe acid rain—who could say? It was high time for them to be cut, anyway.

As I write this, eight years after the storm, the dozen or so pines that survived still appear to be thriving. I cherish each one. I check in the spring to see if all of them have survived the winter. So far they have, even though the loss of the trees that used to surround them should have made them more vulnerable to high winds than ever.

But the survival of these trees doesn't mean Hank Benson was wrong. Maybe they were the healthiest ones, and that's why the storm failed to topple them. In fact, most likely he was right, and one of these days they'll keel over.

If I'd been aware before the storm that the trees were starting to show signs of rot, would I have had them cut? "Harvested" them, as they say up here? I doubt it. I'm not that much of a Vermonter. Maybe I'm a just another fool of a flatlander, as my neighbors probably think.

I suppose I'd have clung to them and hoped for the best. I loved the woods, and love is not rational.

The Wildflower Meadow

The half-acre field beside the road lay bare and brown. As the snow receded and the sun warmed the earth, wild grasses and ferns sprang up in the neighboring fields with their usual abandon, and brambles, Tartarian honeysuckle, and native filbert unfurled their tightly-packed leaves, turning the gray world green. But in the half-acre field no growing thing appeared that spring, except for a few sparse shoots of milkweed and goldenrod.

After last summer's violent storm, which destroyed our woods and leveled a century-old stand of white pine, the logger had made his "stage" in the field. There he had dragged the fallen trees, three or four at a time chained behind the heavy skidder, to be piled and stacked until they were trucked to the sawmill. The stage had been in use for a couple of months, while the logger cleared out the mass of blowdown.

The dragging of the logs and the passing and repassing of the skidder had scoured and churned and lacerated the half-acre field. The wild seeds of the meadow

plants had been pulverized, or buried too deep to germinate. Even the roots of stout perennials like dandelion
and burdock seemed to have been dealt a mortal blow.
Baking in the sun, the bare earth, criss-crossed with
tracks, lay as dark and crusted as a scab over a wound.

The stage was still littered here and there with piles of
pulpwood, logs too short to be sold for lumber and useful only for grinding up into paper or chipboard.
Pulpwood wasn't worth much, which was why the logger had left the piles behind. I ought to have kept after
him until he took them away, only I was too disheart-
ened by the larger chaos that surrounded us. Every time
we stepped out the door we saw the lifeless acres of
stumps left behind by the storm.

The half-acre field was located just beyond the driveway that led from the road to the house. I saw it every
time I got in the car or drove up the road. I waited for
the field to turn green, sure that this wouldn't take long;
weeds shot up in my flowerbeds every time I turned my
back—why not out there, where the exposed earth
looked so inviting? But time went by and nothing happened. The nakedness of the field was the final insult,
added to the injury of the destruction of our woods. I felt
aggrieved whenever I looked at it.

That spring I refused to work in the garden. Gardening
seemed futile. Another blow from Nature could come
along at any moment to mock my efforts—a late snow, a
hailstorm, a flood. I sulked. The weeds grew tall, then
taller.

But the task had to be faced. One day, grimly, I took out a tarp, spread it on the ground in front of a perennial bed, narrowed my focus to that small, familiar patch of earth, and settled into the timeless rhythm of weeding. As I worked my way down the bed, a feeling of comfort began to seep into my bones.

The previous spring the pulmonaria had performed superbly. Pulmonaria, or lungwort, is a low, spreading plant that blooms early in spring and has the odd characteristic that its small flowers are pink when they open and then turn blue. In the past it was used to treat diseases of the lung, hence the name. Last year when the flowers had finished blooming, I had dug up the plant and divided it.

I always enjoy dividing perennials. It still amazes me that you can pry a big plant out of the ground, poke your fingers or a knife right into the heart of the rootball, pry and hack it into pieces, and then wander about the garden tucking the pieces into the ground here and there, all without doing the least harm to the life-force of the plant. I can't remember ever losing any divisions, except in the sense that by the following spring I often forget where I've planted them. I do my dividing while surrounded by pails of water into which I plop the pieces of the plant after surgery, thus minimizing the time the roots are exposed to the drying air. Misty days when there is a barely perceptible drizzle are best for this job, as for any kind of transplanting. When divided under such conditions, most perennials will hardly skip a beat. But in spite of what the books say, you can transplant and divide perennials at any time, even on a sunny day in midsummer. It just takes more follow-up. You must

shade the divisions (I cut spruce boughs and stick them
in the ground to provide cover), and of course you must
water them daily for a week or longer. Waiting for a
misty day is better.

Slowly, I moved along the bed. I pulled out a clump of
weeds that had been crowding one of the pulmonaria divisions. The small shoot had grown into a lusty rosette
of fresh green leaves spotted with silver. As I weeded
around it, the plant seemed to expand, like a broody hen
fluffing up its feathers, and then settle back against its
nest of newly plumped earth.

I like to weed using a small, claw-shaped hand culti-
vator to loosen the earth, while with my left hand I take
a good handful of weeds and wiggle and pull them free
without harming the nearby perennials. If the day is
sunny and the weeds are small, they can be left on the
bed to shrivel, returning their nutrients to the soil while
providing a bit of mulch. If the weeds are larger I toss
them on the tarp, to be emptied into the compost bin for
eventual return, by a more circuitous route, to the garden. Later in the summer I often weed with a long-
handled hoe, which is easier on the back; but the first
weeding of the season is best done with a hand cultiva-
tor because desirable seedlings have a way of popping up
in unexpected places, and you have to be on the alert for
them. Sometimes even an experienced gardener must
look closely to distinguish them from the weeds.

I was uncovering quite a bountiful crop of seedlings—
too many, in fact. The previous year, overwhelmed by the
cleanup after the storm, I had neglected to cut back the
perennials after they had bloomed. The seeds had ma-
tured on the plants and fallen to earth, where some had
germinated.

Seedlings are Nature's way of giving the perennial gardener a bonus. Often this handout is too much of a good thing, especially when it comes to foxgloves and poppies, which must be ruthlessly weeded out or, rather, thinned; I love both of them and always keep at least a few. Strictly speaking, foxgloves are biennials (although they sometimes linger a bit longer than two years) and poppies are annuals, but both reappear so reliably in my garden that I tend to think of them as perennials. The true perennials are more chary with their seedlings, especially if you cut the plants back after flowering, which in normal years I do. The few seedlings that pop up anyway will be greeted as a welcome surprise instead of a nuisance.

I am always glad to come upon seedlings of euphorbia and perennial geranium. I can generally find a place for them, if only in the holding bed where I grow surplus perennials in rows for future projects, or to give to friends. I love the way the golden bracts of the euphorbia—bracts are not really flowers, but the plant's upper leaves—glow in the cool sunlight of early spring. In my garden, euphorbia always "blooms" at the same time as a certain pale lavender creeping phlox, and I like to plant the two together for a glorious spring picture. As for perennial geraniums, they, too, are fine plants, whether in the front of a bed or spilling over a stone wall. One characteristic shared by both plants is the beautiful, shapely mounds of foliage they form, so that even when they have finished blooming they more than justify the space they take in the garden. In fact, the first time I was ever attracted to euphorbia was in a friend's garden in midsummer. "What's that wonderful foliage plant?" I asked him, thinking it as fine as a hosta. He told me the name, I bought a specimen, and the next spring it dazzled me with the brilliance of its sunny bracts. Since then, I've been hooked on it. There are many different euphorbias—thousands, in fact, all over the world. They are named after Euphorbus, a physician of the 1st century A.D., perhaps because several species have medicinal value. Others, like cassava, are food plants, and still others are poisonous, such as the South African toxicodendron, one of the most lethal plants known. All of these are related only distantly to the Euphorbia epithymoides, or cushion spurge, in my garden, a plant that is perfectly benign, as far as I know.

As for perennial geraniums, these should not be confused with the heat-loving, stiff, so-called geraniums (actually they are pelargoniums) that are grown in pots on the window sill. Although these are related to perennial geraniums, the latter are larger, more graceful plants with many small flowers, and perfectly hardy even in northern New England. I grow some of the "better" varieties like Johnson's Blue and Wargrave Pink, yet I confess to a special fondness for the old-fashioned magenta kind, which many gardeners find harsh and strident; it is definitely the most vigorous grower, even if you never get around to fertilizing it. For years now I have cherished two fine, bushy mounds of it growing on either side of the granite steps that lead to my front door. This is the door that in Vermont houses is hardly ever opened, for most people prefer to use the kitchen door; in fact, in some houses the front door is kept permanently sealed with plastic or plywood, an inelegant but effective solution to the problem of winter draughts.

Even though I had been remiss the year before, I came upon only a few baby geraniums and euphorbia.

What I did find in extravagant abundance were lupine seedlings. These were the common blue lupine, a handsome plant with tall, stiff spikes of pea-shaped flowers and pretty leaves with narrow "fingers" radiating from a central point. The rather restricted color range of light to dark blue, with an occasional white or pink thrown in for variety, can't compare with the amazing, chromatic fantasies of the Russell hybrid lupines, which were developed by a plantsman who dedicated his life to the task. Nevertheless, I still admire the old-fashioned kind, which thrives in Vermont.

What was I to do with the lupine seedlings? There were dozens, maybe hundreds, all crowded together; I wouldn't know how many until I had finished weeding the bed.

Lupines are members of the pea family, so it is not surprising that the pea-shaped flowers are followed by long, narrow pods containing large, pea-like seeds. The pods are hairy, and as they ripen they turn the silvery gray of weathered barn boards and split apart, the two halves twisting into corkscrews and revealing three to six hard, round seeds. These are tough in every sense of the word and superbly equipped for survival in our part of Vermont, with its moist, acid soil, cool nights, abundant rainfall, and freezing winters with plenty of snow.

As I weeded my way down the bed, it gradually dawned on me that just about every seed my lupines had produced last summer had germinated. Feeling like the Sorcerer's Apprentice, I stared at all those eager infants, aghast. What was I to do with them? I had always been totally incapable of discarding lupine seedlings. The plants were so tall, so elegant, and the babies so sweet, so helpless—it went against the grain. Because of this weakness of mine, the kind a gardener shouldn't have, I always took particular care to cut back the lupines after they had bloomed, allowing only a spike or two to go to seed to provide replacements. "Perennial" does not mean immortal, and although some plants, like peonies, may live for generations, others, lupines among them, are apt to fade out after a few years. The few seedlings that popped up could replace weakened plants, and any extras could be potted up and given to friends.

But last year I had slipped up, and as a result there were far too many. Transplanting some of them—there wouldn't be room for all—to the holding bed until I decided what to do with them was not an option. Lupines have taproots and resent being transplanted, even when young; I've never dared to move them when mature. No, wherever I decided to put them, there they would remain.

I took a break for lunch. After I washed the dishes, I drove down to the general store and picked up a few groceries. On my return, my eyes fell on the half-acre field, bare as ever. It was then that inspiration struck.

Suppose I moved the seedlings to the field?

Some years earlier I had flirted with the idea of creating a wildflower meadow, egged on by my cousin Joyce, who was infatuated with wildflowers but didn't want to go to the trouble and expense of making a wildflower meadow on her own land. She thought I should do it.

I admit I was intrigued. Wildflower meadows were and still are very much in vogue. Although Joyce seemed

to think all I needed to do was buy a few pounds of wildflower seed and skip merrily over a field scattering it
about, perhaps while wearing a chaplet of daisies in my
hair—she didn't mention the chaplet, but it was im-
plied—I had a feeling it wouldn't be that easy. The
meadow was already crammed with grasses, goldenrod,
milkweed, daisies, bindweed, asters, black-eyed Susan,
and purple vetch, all madly elbowing each other out of
the way. How was a genuine "wildflower seed" ever to
reach the dirt, let alone a patch of it large enough to
grow in?

I read a couple of articles about wildflower meadows
and came away convinced that making one was a big job.
First of all, you had to plow up a field. Having grown up
in an apartment instead of on a farm, I find the mere
idea of plowing a major psychological barrier. Next, you
had to rake the field thoroughly to remove as many
weeds as possible (I hate raking, it's too much like
sweeping), saturate the area with weed killer (I hate
chemicals), and wait until next spring (I really hate waiting), when you would give the area another shot of
weed-killer to be on the safe side. Then you could start
planting.

Alternatively, you could dig individual holes in a field,
and purchase or raise wildflowers to plant in them—the
"plug method"—but having already tried to dig an occasional hole in the matted turf of a field, I wasn't eager to
repeat the experience on a large scale.

All in all, I could see this wasn't my kind of project, although I didn't like to disappoint my cousin. I told her I
already had a wildflower meadow containing goldenrod
and milkweed and daisies, et cetera, et cetera, but she

wasn't satisfied. That kind of field didn't count. She didn't say so out loud, but she's a relative and I knew what she was thinking. Everybody in Vermont had that kind of field. It didn't look like the wildflower meadows in books.

One Saturday we drove to a nursery that specialized in wildflowers. It had a shop where seeds, books, tools, and garden ornaments were sold, and out back an extensive wildflower meadow with a path running through the middle. Joyce and I browsed through the store and then walked down the path. The meadow was indeed lovely. It contained the same flowers that grew in my field, except with a higher concentration of flowers to grass; also it was liberally sprinkled with pink, cerise, and white cosmos, as well as red poppies like the ones I'd seen in the fields in France and Switzerland. The cosmos and poppies looked wonderful, but of course they would only last for one season, as they were annuals. Joyce bought some Sweet William seed she wanted to try planting in a problem area behind her house. I bought nothing and left the nursery feeling confused.

I find the concept "wildflower meadow" elusive, perhaps because the definition of a wildflower is itself far from clear. Personally, I wouldn't put cosmos, Sweet William, or poppies from Flanders field in that category, at least not in Vermont, although of course they all grow wild—are native—somewhere in the world. But has a plant no right to be called a wildflower unless it is native? What about Queen Anne's lace and daisies, which were brought to this country by early settlers?

There are people who believe the only plants in a region that can be considered truly "wild" are those that predate the arrival of the white man in North America. Such plants can be hard to find now, having been pushed out of their original habitats by later, more vigorous arrivals that escaped from colonial gardens or were carried over from Europe in ships' ballast. These purists seem to consider the presence of the pretty parvenus immoral and by great efforts have managed to eradicate them from a certain number of acres, restoring them to their aboriginal condition. This proceeding seems a bit drastic to me, not that I think such historical restoration projects shouldn't be carried out. The world needs a certain number of original thinkers to come up with bold new ideas that jolt us out of our complacent ruts. It is only when they start trying to make everyone agree with them that I get nervous. Luckily there is always a tremendous amount of apathy around, which makes it hard for zealots to take over.

To me, the Vermont fields in their usual state, whether you want to call it "wild" or not, are beautiful, and sometimes they offer a whole new perspective on plants that I tend to think of as troublesome weeds because I am always pulling them out of my flowerbeds. An upland meadow ablaze with dandelions in early spring, or an undulating field of goldenrod in the fall, gives one a new appreciation for these common plants.

But from time to time I pass certain fields that give me a special shock of pleasure. One is filled with purple fireweed, which does grow wild in Vermont, but not usually *en masse* as in this field; another contains chiefly gloriosa daisies, garden perennials that look like giant black-eyed Susans. Both fields adjoin houses and have obviously been created deliberately. The fireweed and the gloriosas have persisted for years, although nobody seems to weed them and other wildlings grow among them. As far as I'm concerned, that makes these fields wildflower meadows—and I think many people would agree.

I also know a dirt road where red bee balm, another garden perennial, rambles all over the shoulder for several hundred feet, holding its own against the usual Queen Anne's lace, goldenrod, and so forth, offering an unexpected treat to strollers and passing motorists. Somebody must have put it there.

And then there are the lupine meadows. Whenever I drive the twenty miles to Montpelier I pass several of them. Each year I look forward eagerly to seeing them in bloom, and from the time the budding spears come into view in early summer until the fading flowers go to seed a month later, I slow my car to a crawl every time I drive by. The sweep of blue, dotted here and there with pink and white, is breathtaking, and the soft colors suit the misty Vermont landscape perfectly.

When I first saw these lupine meadows I assumed they were natural; but as I learned more about gardening, I realized they must be man-made. I thought no less of them for that. If anything, the gratitude I felt toward their unknown creators increased my pleasure in those eye-filling sweeps of color. The meadows seemed to be self-perpetuating. Over the years they slowly expanded, growing even more magnificent. I noticed that they were mowed after the lupines had bloomed, which seemed to be all the care they required. If I ever had a wildflower meadow, I thought, that would be the kind for me. Yet I never seriously considered making one. The task seemed beyond my scope.

Then the storm came along, altering our land. The following spring, the unexpected confluence of a naked field and a bumper crop of lupine seedlings—both of them side effects of the storm—jogged the part of my brain where the memory of the lupine meadows was stored. Why not try to create one—what did I have to lose?

I set to work, using a modification of the "plug" method. Digging holes in the bare earth for the seedlings was easy, and could even be done with a trowel. I started planting next to the road and worked my way back into the field, setting the seedlings at random and leaving plenty of space between them. With such a large area to cover, I knew I wouldn't have enough seedlings; I hoped the plants would fill in and spread. I also planned to collect seed from the lupines in my flowerbeds later that summer, as well as from other plants that might be sturdy enough to fend for themselves: tiger lilies, purple coneflower, gloriosa daisies, and hollyhock. I would throw the seeds on the field and hope they grew. This whole thing was an experiment—it would be interesting to see what happened.

Once I had planted the seedlings, I gave each one a drink. I had brought pails of water, for my hose was too short to reach the field. Then I stepped out on the road and surveyed my work. It did not look impressive. From where I stood, the field seemed huge and the puny seedlings pathetic. Still, I'd made a start.

Summers in Vermont are cool and moist. Even on sunny days there may be brief periods of rain; mountains make for changeable weather. From my seat on the porch I can watch the clouds roll in, always coming from the west over the ridge across the road. They can cover a

blue sky in twenty minutes. Then rain begins to fall.
Sometimes it lasts all day, but often the clouds keep on
sailing east until, before long, the sun comes out again.
The locals say, "If you don't like the weather in Vermont,
wait five minutes."

I was counting on rain to give the seedlings a good
start. Unfortunately, no sooner had I finished planting
than a prolonged drought set in. I carried pails of water
out to the field and watered the drooping seedlings as
the blazing sun baked the field. Belatedly, I ran around
poking leafy branches into the ground to provide a bit of
shade. I prayed for rain. I grew depressed.

The days, and even the nights, were so hot that there
was a run on the electric fans that had been gathering dust
in the back of the general store. By the time I tried to buy
one they were all gone, and Cousin Joyce, who often goes
to New York, had to bring me one from Zabar's.

Hoses were sold out, too. I managed to find some in
Montpelier to lengthen my hose enough for it to reach
into the field. That helped a little—at least I didn't have
to carry pails—but since our water came from a spring I
had to use it sparingly. Our neighbors' wells were running dry, and I didn't want to drain our cistern.

I didn't see how the lupines could survive. They were
finicky about being transplanted under the best of cir-
cumstances, and despite my efforts, the drought was
stressing them severely. Yet they clung to life—and finally it rained.

The lupine meadow is eight years old now and thriving.
It can't compare in size or impact to the ones I still look

forward to seeing when I drive to Montpelier, but it is self-sufficient and growing larger. It hasn't yet filled the area bounded by the road, the drainage ditch along the driveway, and the strip of woods that was spared by the storm, but perhaps in time it will.

The first year or two I transplanted odds and ends from the garden into the field, most successfully a few clumps of red bee balm into a spot near the road. For some reason, these grew spectacularly, and they are twice as tall as the ones in the garden. As for the purple cone-flowers, gloriosa daisies, and hollyhocks I planted, they seem to be dying out. They still send up a flower here and there, enough to vary a meadow bouquet. But the field belongs to the lupines, and to the daisies and gold-enrod that have come up between them.

In late summer when the lupines go to seed, I cut the spikes and strew them around the edges of the field. This lazy-man's method is surprisingly successful. Some of the seeds work their way down into the earth and grow into new plants without any further attention from me.

My neighbors have begun to notice the field, and when it is in bloom they tell me, during our encounters at the general store, "Flowers lookin' good."

One day I happened to look out of an upstairs win-dow and saw a car parked on the shoulder of the road next to the field. As I stood there wondering whose it was, a couple got out and started gathering lupines. Another time a woman with a spade and a bucket pro-ceeded to dig up a plant. "That won't grow," I thought, not sure whether to be indignant or amused. The red bee balm has made a hit, too. People come to my door and, observing local etiquette, ask permission to dig up a plant. I say "Yes, but please take only one." Others don't ask, but just wade into the field with their shovels. When this happens, I tell myself that I wanted to create a wildflower meadow and apparently I've succeeded.

I have a natural tendency to be a planner. I make lists, I set goals, I draw floor plans. Before I put up a kitchen shelf I measure the cereal boxes and the soup cans with a ruler. In this I am like my mother, who took the term "domestic engineer" seriously. My planning tendencies were strengthened during the time when I was running a household and raising four children, while also going to graduate school, acquiring a profession, and eventually practicing it. I could never have done all this without planning. But in the process, spontaneity drained out of my life. Once that had happened it wasn't easy to get it back, although I missed it more than I knew.

In a way, it surprises me that I do so little advance planning in the garden nowadays. I've read books on landscape architecture, the kind that urge you to get out the graph paper and draw diagrams of beds filled with amoeba shapes representing "drifts" of different kinds of flowers. I resist this advice. Garden planning, like family planning, takes some of the spontaneity out of the act. Now that my life has room in it for the unexpected, I don't care to chase it away.

Allowing the nature of the land to be my guide, I stick tawny daylilies, which will grow anywhere, into the thin, dry soil over a ledge. I curve a border around an old butternut tree, dig a bed in front of a stone wall that just happens to be there, and take advantage of a swamp to make a pond. With particular delight, I welcome happy accidents. When the accidents seem less than happy—like a bare field and a surfeit of lupine seedlings—I try to accept what nature hands me and work with it.

Spontaneity has flowed back into my life, and with it a greater sense of freedom. This may seem to be a paradox. Shouldn't one feel most autonomous when imposing one's own design, conceived at one's desk with a ruler and compass, on the natural world? Maybe so, but I find it more enjoyable to take my cue from nature. I would rather collaborate than be completely in charge. This is when I experience, to the fullest extent, the inner freedom that comes from being in harmony with nature.

I know that after I am gone, the weeds will swallow up my garden within a few years. The path I built will be invaded by blackberries and close up, not too long after we cease to mow it. Even the pond will fill with silt eventually and revert to swampland.

But the lupine meadow can take care of itself. The topsoil of the field rests on hardpan, and trees don't seem to thrive there, so I don't even mow once a year to keep the trees from taking over. The lupine meadow, which I did not plan, and which came about almost by accident, will very likely last longer than anything else in my garden.

One Man's Fuchsia

"What are those?" he says. "Wait, wait, don't tell me!" Joe has noticed a clump of pansies. They have been blooming beside the kitchen door since I planted them in May, and it is now July. He raises a finger to keep me from giving him hints, but he needn't worry. I know my part in this ritual. "Don't say anything—they're petunias!" He can tell from my expression that this is not right. "No?" He waves away any correction I may be moved to offer. "Pansies! They're pansies, right?"

"Very good."

He beams. He loves praise. "I knew it started with a 'p'. See? I'm learning." Now he becomes overconfident. He points at a primrose. "Marigold?"

"Uh uh."

"Goldenrod?"

"Nope."

"Well, something yellow, anyway. Am I getting warm!"

I have been married to this man for two-thirds of my life. Shouldn't more of me have rubbed off on him by now? On the other hand, not much theoretical physics has rubbed off on me—in fact, none. "It's a primrose," I say. "They're tricky."

"Ah. Another 'p.'" Joe's mind is constantly organizing and classifying in ways that remain mysterious to me. "Primrose, primrose—" He is trying to commit the name to memory, but both of us know he will fail. It seems he just can't—or won't—retain such details, much as he would like to please me. Anyway, if he succeeded he would have to stop playing this game, which he likes because it reminds him of how cute he is. Joe has been cute since he was a tyke in Vienna, where women would tousle his golden curls and tell him that all the girls in America would love him because of his curly hair. Meanwhile his father was standing in line at the American embassy to get a visa and save his family from the Holocaust. In this, ultimately, he succeeded, or Joe would not be standing with me at this moment, trying to memorize the name of a flower.

Joe bears few visible scars of the Holocaust, except that he will help any refugee who comes his way and cannot bear to see movies about Nazis. There are subtler traces, such as the anxiety he shows at the prospect of being separated from me when we are in train stations or airports. But in general he is a lively man, tells a lot of jokes, and is kind to the point of saintliness except now and then with me (but I am his wife and a man can't keep to that standard all the time). His secretaries weep on his shoulder, and his students write him letters that begin "Dearest Dr. Sucher." Not dear. Dearest.

By now Joe has lost most of his hair, although his inner conviction of his cuteness remains undimmed. The few flyaway strands that persist are gray mixed with white. They tend to stand straight up as if electrified, like Einstein's.

People like to send Joe pictures and posters of Einstein, and there is one he has hung on the wall of his small, messy study in Vermont. In it the great scientist gazes thoughtfully into space with his dark, lustrous eyes. The words on the poster say: "I want to know God's thoughts. All the rest are details." Joe doesn't like to be bothered with everyday details, either. Maybe this is because he is always trying to wrestle them, mentally, into a coherent, logical whole. They resist, which he finds frustrating. Often when I see the poster I think of Mrs. Einstein. There is a story that when a reporter asked her if she understood Einstein's theory of relativity, she replied, "No, but I understand Einstein."

Joe is still saying, "Primrose, primrose," but rather mechanically. His thoughts have drifted off where I cannot follow. I am used to this. Something has caught his attention and he is cogitating, perhaps about the work he is doing. After a while he may produce a new theory. As long as I've known him, theorizing has come naturally to him. I am drawn more to the particular than the general, so we balance each other. Sometimes the theories Joe comes up with about everyday matters—he states them as facts, as if trying to slip them by me without being challenged—strike me as wrong to the point of absurdity, which makes me wonder a bit about his physics theories. But they must be all right, because he is always being asked to give talks.

We prepare to embark on a little walk around the garden. We seldom do this, because Joe hates being bitten by bugs, which he claims happens more to him than to ordinary people, and with worse consequences—"huge welts," he says, displaying and counting them to see if he has broken any records.

He doesn't hate bugs per se; in fact, they interest him. Sometimes, quite excitedly, he will call me over to examine one, perhaps a large spider spinning a web on the outside of a windowpane (the ideal situation), and I sense in him an inclination to reach for a pad and start making notes. He doesn't, because he's not a biologist but a physicist; yet the scientific instinct is always there. However, in his work Joe doesn't deal directly with nature—not with gases under pressure or particles that leave tracks of their passing on photographic plates, let alone spiders or pansies. He keeps his distance, leaving such matters to experimentalists. His job is simply to think about things, mathematically.

In this marriage, I am the experimentalist.

We are almost ready for our tour of the garden. Joe has changed into shoes with arch supports. Now he sprays himself thoroughly with Deep Woods OFF, and we head for the nearest flower bed. He is filled with admiration and praise for my efforts. He bends down to sniff the flowers, making no distinction between those that are fragrant and those that are not, for he retains little memory of the last time we walked here. He is a tabula rasa, savoring the experience with the freshness of a child. "What's this one called?" he keeps asking, and as always I tell him. Iris, lily, malva, delphinium, phlox: the names fall around us like autumn leaves and drift away on the breeze. Sometimes his expression grows abstracted, but then he pulls himself back to the garden and says, "What's this one called?"

Joe has no context in which to fix the names of the flowers. They remain isolated facts, mere oddments of data. He has never worked with flowers, thought about their needs, puzzled over where to plant them so that their requirements will be met, fought for their survival against pests, weeds, and drought, he has never blackened his nails in the dirt.

Yet there are certain kinds of mundane details he does notice. In the days of our courtship—I was eighteen and he was twenty—when we wandered the streets of Manhattan hand-in-hand, he would suddenly say something like, "Look! That's the sum of two squares!"

"What?"

He would point to a car and explain that the number on the license plate was the sum of two squares—or a square and a cube, or a Fibonacci number, or whatever.

It had never occurred to me that anyone might notice the numbers on license plates. But they leaped out at him—all numbers did, and still do. The only other person I've known who noticed license plates automatically was a policeman, because he had been trained to be on the lookout for stolen cars.

Once when I was extremely busy I asked Joe to deadhead the petunias. Every summer I grow petunias in a sunny corner of the porch: a sumptuous mixture of pinks and purples and white (the white is crucial) planted in a big, old-fashioned tub. Because Joe often spends time on the porch, which is securely screened and has a sofa conducive to naps—and more importantly because it was he who painted the big tub white—he has developed an awareness of these petunias and makes spontaneous comments about them, even though their name may slip his mind.

I gave him a pair of scissors and explained the simple theory behind deadheading: the faded flowers are removed so that they won't go to seed; if they do, the plant stops producing flowers. He grasped the concept and was in fact quite intrigued, asking me how I knew this. Had I tried not doing it? Had I studied several petunia plants, deadheading some but not others so I could observe the relative rate of flower production? In other words, had I conducted a controlled experiment?

I said, "No, I haven't," adding rather testily, for I was in a hurry, "these things are known."

"But don't you want to make sure? Deadheading these flowers could take a lot of time."

"Please just do it."

Looking skeptical, he said he would.

When I returned I found he had removed all the dead petunia blossoms. He had also removed every single bud. "Oh, my God!" I said. "You've cut the buds off!"

"I what?"

"You cut the buds off!" With difficulty I restrained myself from adding, "you idiot!" "Now they won't bloom again for ages!"

"You never told me there was a difference—"

"My God, can't you tell life from death?" I was really

irritated. "It shouldn't have to be explained! Do you think anyone ever explained it to me?"

He looked hurt. He had been expecting praise. I felt a twinge of guilt, as if he were a child.

Several years ago, things changed. Not much—"incrementally," Joe would say—yet enough to be worthy of note.

One spring we paid a visit to Farmer Katz, who lives down the road. We always drop by soon after our arrival in Vermont to buy hanging plants for the porch. At one time we also bought our vegetables from Farmer Katz, whose first name is Gary. Then his Japanese-American wife, Vicki, started selling a few flower baskets, perennials, and flats of annuals on the side. I seem to remember that Gary was a bit caustic about this, at the time. He is a smart Jewish guy from New Jersey who was a chemist before we knew him; back when he rebelled against the nine-to-five, moved to Vermont, and became a farmer, flowers probably didn't play much part in his dream, if any. But Vicki, beneath her shy manner, is smart, artistic, very good with the customers, and a hard worker. She persisted, and after a few years the flowers turned out to be more profitable than the vegetables and were edging the peppers and eggplants out of the greenhouse. Now flowers form the major part of the business, although a field is still planted with squash, cucumbers, corn, potatoes, and beets, and Farmer Katz is still famed for his tomatoes, which monopolize a section of one greenhouse. "People up here would kill for a decent tomato," he growls, to conceal the pride he feels. In the cool north country with its short growing season, this is almost literally true.

The number of greenhouses has now grown to four, mostly filled with flowers, for Gary keeps building more to keep up with the demand. There are flats of impatiens, petunias, marigolds, cosmos (old standbys as well as newer varieties the Katzes have thought worthy of a trial), and sweet-smelling pansies and even sweeter alyssum, both the white and purple kinds. Overhead dangle the hanging baskets, which the Katzes believe in stuffing generously with plants and fertilizing richly, so that they will burst into glorious fountains of bloom no prospective buyer can resist.

I was conferring with Vicki in the open shed over a table filled with plants. We were admiring a flat of pastel pansies and discussing whether their delicate shades of apricot and cream might be too subtle to show up well in the garden, and whether it might be better to plant them in a big pot, where they could be admired at close range. Joe had wandered off into the greenhouses to look for Gary, whom he considers something of a kindred spirit because they come from similar backgrounds, and Gary is, or was, a scientist.

Then for some reason Joe noticed that the upper reaches of the greenhouse were crowded with hanging fuchsias (Gary had told him their name), and that they were absolutely spectacular. He said something like, "I have to show these to Dorothy. Maybe she should buy one."

"Whaddya mean?" Gary demanded. "Why do you have to ask *her*? Don't you have a right to your own fuchsia?"

Joe told me about this conversation a few minutes later. "I'm thinking of buying a fuchsia," he said, and waited for my reaction.

"That's good," I said.

"You have to see these fuchsias."

"Okay."

"You have to help me pick one out."

"Wait a minute. I thought you said this was your fuchsia. You pick it out."

"But there's a lot of different kinds."

"Just take one you like."

He looked worried. "It's hard to tell which is best. They're all nice."

"Then you can't lose."

He shook his head. He has trouble making decisions. He needs to feel sure that he has come up with the best and only solution to the problem. I've tried to tell him that many problems don't have a best solution—what's important is just to decide and stop dithering. But he is not convinced.

I went with him to see the fuchsias, and they were sensational. There were red and white ones, with flowers like tiny ballerinas. There were red and pink ones, and pink and purple doubles with ruffled skirts, and red and purple combinations, and pink and lavender. It was still early in the season, and the best ones hadn't yet been snatched away by eager buyers. Poor Joe—making a choice was going to be torture. But I was not going to be maneuvered into making it for him.

He gave me a helpless look. "So—what do you think?"

"They're gorgeous."

"But which—"

Arms folded across his chest, Gary stood there, glowering, and waited for me to try—just try!—depriving my poor husband of his masculine prerogatives.

I thought, "You'll have a long wait, my friend," and said nothing.

There was a long silence. Joe wandered along the greenhouse aisles, his eyes cast upward despairingly. Finally he said, "The first thing is to establish some basic principles." He was thinking hard. "For example, is one with a lot of flowers better, or one with less flowers but a lot of buds?" He looked at me and then Gary, to see if he was on the right track.

I nodded. I felt I could go that far; I hate to see a man in misery.

"Okay," he said, and stroked his chin thoughtfully. "But which? This is the problem of delayed gratification—always difficult, of course."

I shifted my weight and leaned back against a plant bench. This might take a while.

"I think—" he said, "More buds! To prolong the enjoyment! That's definitely better. You not only want to enjoy the fuchsia, you want to enjoy it for a long time! Right?"

"Right!" I said. My feet were beginning to hurt.

"Okay!" he said. "We're making progress." He cast his eyes around the greenhouse and sighed. "Now. What kind of fuchsia? This is more difficult. This is a problem of personal taste. All colors are, in a sense, equally good. But!"—I could see he'd had a brainstorm—"It seems reasonable to say, a priori, that more contrast is better than less. That means I should get a red-and-white one!" He looked around at us delightedly.

"Great!" I said. "Take one and let's go home."

"But which one—"

"Come on, man!" Gary said. "Every single plant in this greenhouse is perfect. I guarantee it! Take that one."

"That's the best one?"

Gary unhooked a red-and-white fuchsia with plenty of buds, and thrust it into Joe's hands. "Best, shmest, it's a fuchsia, for God's sake!"

Every summer since then, Joe has had his own fuchsia hanging on our screened porch. Although this gives him much pleasure, it has opened him to a world of cares. The fuchsia has a persistent habit of growing toward the light, which is stronger on one side than the other, and this troubles him, as it makes the shape of the plant uneven. There is such a thing as symmetry in the universe, after all, and he would like his fuchsia to reflect that principle even though he knows that in the more arcane realms of physics the universality of symmetry was disproved some years ago. He is always trying to turn the plant so that it will grow more evenly. I've suggested trimming it, but this strikes him as too drastic.

Joe waters the fuchsia faithfully and has quantified the process: a cup and a half every two days, regardless of the weather. I can't help thinking the plant should be given more water on hot or windy days, but his method works and the fuchsia looks fine. If a leaf or two turns yellow, though, he consults me worriedly. Generally a shot of Rapid-Gro solves the problem. The yellow leaves revert to green, and a few days later there is a surge of new growth, which he notes with fatherly pride.

He has now mastered the art of deadheading, practices it regularly, and no longer has any trouble telling a seedpod from a bud. Once in a while his thoughts wander, and he cuts off a bud by mistake. I tell him this could happen to anyone, but it gives him a terrible pang.

Then there is the question of what to do about the faded blossoms. They keep falling off the plant and landing on the white-painted, built-in bench below, staining the wood when the rain blows in through the screening. Joe has stationed a large glass tray on the bench below the fuchsia to catch most of the fallen flowers. These pile up in gray-brown lumps he considers unesthetic, but not enough for him to make a "special trip" to the trash can. So he leaves them in the glass tray to be dealt with later.

If I ask him, "When, later?" he goes vague on me. "Later" is something like the Uncertainty Principle.

As for the dead flowers that miss the glass tray and drop on the floor, these might as well have fallen into a black hole as far as he is concerned. They are not his responsibility. He has provided a glass tray. If a dead flower declines to use it, so much the worse for it!

Recently we visited Farmer Katz. Vicki greeted us, asked if Joe had come for his annual fuchsia, and when we asked for Gary she sent us off to the furthest greenhouse, saying, "We keep him up there."

As Gary growled a welcome, I noticed that a few strands of gray had crept into his black beard. "Here for your fuchsia?" he said to Joe, who nodded. "Well, you won't need any help, by now you're an expert."

For a while Joe prowled the aisles, looking upward. He said to Gary, "What do you think about this one?"

"What do I think? I think it's perfect. They're all perfect."

"Does it have enough buds? Does this fuchsia have a future?"

There was a silence. "Is that a pun?" said Gary suspiciously.

"There are mosquitoes in this greenhouse. I just got a bite. It's swelling up with relativistic speed here."

"How about this one?" Gary said. He unhooked a red-and-white fuchsia and rehung it where it could be seen more clearly. We studied it. It was outstanding. Waxing positively poetic, Gary stated, "This plant is ample, round, and full."

"Ample, round, and full," Joe echoed thoughtfully. "Or 'ARF'."

Gary's dog, who was lying on the ground, lifted his head and looked around alertly.

I said, "You're talking his language."

With a confidence born of experience, Joe chose the 'ARF' fuchsia. Then, while I picked out cosmos and snapdragons, he and Gary launched into a long discussion of a recent experiment proving, or at least strongly suggesting, that the neutrino has mass.

The Path

I am always trying to lose weight, and everything I try works, but only for a while. Some years ago this ongoing quest led me to a spa in North Carolina where I began, for the first time, to actually enjoy exercise. I especially liked the walks I took on a gravel trail that wound through the woods behind the buildings. The trail had wooden footbridges over a sluggish creek that looked suspiciously like a drainage ditch, a circular loop you could go around and around until your willpower gave out, and a bench at the highest point where you could sit and catch your breath. I liked the damp, woodsy smell on the trail and the quietness broken only by my gasps as I labored up the hills, pausing now and then to take my pulse (if I could find it) and see if I had reached what the exercise counselor told me was my "target heart range."

After a couple of weeks of walking through these woods—which were rather uninteresting, consisting mostly of skinny southern pines and a few ferns—it occurred to me that I might try to make a similar path in Vermont. Our northern woods, with their sugar maples, dark spruce and balsam, stately white pines, lush beds of fern, ground pine, trillium, and an occasional wild orchid, were so much more varied and fascinating. And surely if I had a path on my own property I would walk every day. I wouldn't have to pay good money to go to a spa and do it.

The idea of our path had been born, but for years it remained dormant. I continued walking on the road, when I walked at all. I was caught up in other projects. From time to time I thought about making a path, but the ground in the woods was rough and would have to be leveled before I could walk there briskly. In some places the underbrush was dense and bristly, and in others large stones reared up that might have to be moved. I filed away the idea of a path in the back of my mind, along with other fantasies that would probably never reach fruition because they were too difficult and expensive to carry out.

Then came the storm that leveled our pinewoods. For a year or two afterward I couldn't bring myself to climb the hill to see if the wounded earth had begun to heal. When I finally began to do so, it seemed natural to follow the "logging road," the track left by the machine of the logger who had hauled away the fallen trees. But the surface was treacherous underfoot and littered with limbs the logger had cut away so he could drag the trunks down to the main road. I picked my way carefully, using a walking stick.

The logging road climbed the hill in a gradual, pleasing, not-too-steep curve. It ran along parallel to the ridge, and then dipped down again in the general direction of the house before petering out. Most of the original undergrowth had been scraped away by the logging operations, and thorny canes of wild blackberries were beginning to spring up, with here and there a poplar shoot. In the natural succession of regrowth that follows a catastrophe in a New England forest, brambles and sun-loving trees such as pin cherries and poplars are always the first to appear. Poplar, especially, was already sprouting in abundance.

Vermonters call poplar "popple," and they detest it. Popple, they claim, is good for nothing. You can't build with it or burn it, and it can quickly take over a field. Yet it is a pretty tree, with its smooth gray trunk and delicate, tremulous leaves. Poplar has its uses, as in the making of toys and wooden buckets, where the lightness of the wood is an asset. Its fast growth checks soil erosion, a valuable trait following the destruction of a forest. Since the storm, I'd noticed more silt than usual washing into our pond. As the poplars grew, their roots would help hold the remaining soil in place.

We had owned a graceful stand of poplars, about twenty-five feet in diameter, where the slender trunks had grown so thickly that an adult could barely slip between them. The storm had knocked the trees down, stacking the trunks parallel on the ground as neatly as pencils in a box. This stand had seemed to be a grove of separate trees, but since poplars sucker freely, springing up from the wandering roots yards or further—sometimes much further—from the mother plant, it is possible the entire grove was really one tree. I have read about a poplar that covers an area of several acres; it is said to be the largest living thing on earth.

Because of the storm, the ideal time to make a walking path had presented itself. The logging road already existed. Now if only the surface could be cleared and smoothed, and the road extended a short distance, and made to curve downhill (or was the slope too steep?) and come out near the house, forming a loop . . .

It seemed a big project, and I'd have liked to talk it over with my grandfather. He was a carpenter and a builder by trade, and had known, or so it had seemed to me when I was young, all there was to know about construction. The path I envisioned would be almost half a mile long and pass through meadow, woodland, and the area of destruction left by the storm. Where was I to start? I was beginning to feel some urgency, for the brambles springing up on the logging road would soon close into an impenetrable thicket.

"Get yourself a bulldozer."

Of course. That's the first thing Grandpa would have said.

I have a passion for bulldozers. It began when I was eight years old, on a day when my grandfather had resolved to clear a piece of land behind his summer house in the Catskills. The two of us spent much of that day standing side by side, arms folded across our chests in classic supervisory stance, watching as the bulldozer he had hired dragged trees out of the way and uprooted stumps. At intervals he exclaimed, "A vonderful machine!" He was a refugee from the pogroms of Russia and had never lost his heavy accent. "It would take a man a week to do what he can do in a day! Maybe two men! Maybe a month, even!"

The endless loop of the massive caterpillar treads moved the machine powerfully forward, crushing all obstacles, as the blade knocked down trees and shoved them all the way to the end of the clearing. Then the machine would back up, blade dragging, and smooth the ground until it was perfectly level. I had been reading in our tattered set of the *Book of Knowledge* about the building of the pyramids, and I grasped at once why my grandfather marveled: machines like this had made a difference to the course of human history.

Fifty years had passed since that day. I still loved bulldozers, and my grandfather had never ceased to stand beside me, although half of that time he had been dead. Now he was in my thoughts more than usual. I wished he were there in the flesh to advise me, but I would just have to manage on my own. I supposed I could; I was his granddaughter. Still, it would have been nice—make that "vonderful"—to hear his voice.

I began to ask around, and before long I found a contractor in the village. Dexter Lewis was an older man who had recently retired from the town road crew. He owned a neat, maneuverable machine that could be used as both a bulldozer and a backhoe, since it had a blade in front and a scoop in back. One morning he came over to my house to walk the proposed route of the path with me. We headed for the vegetable patch where the path was to begin. I was hoping to shame myself into weeding the vegetables more often if I had to confront them on a regular basis. My heart was with the flower beds, and the vegetable patch always looked like a neglected stepchild. Once the path was built, this would change. I would change. I would have no trouble polishing off two boring tasks simultaneously. I would pull weeds and at the same time—especially when the weeds were in the further rows—do some of those "stretches" the instructor at the spa had urged me to include in my exercise program. I felt a surge of fitness at the thought of it.

From the vegetable patch we set out across the meadow. The ground was soggy because of a spring, and we agreed that the contractor would dig a ditch to carry off the water. As for the excavated dirt, he would spread it on the path, raising it high enough to stay firm and dry in all seasons. The path would run alongside the ditch and curve around an ancient apple tree that looked half dead yet put out an annual crop of golf ball-size apples that made great jelly. Crossing the meadow the path would be S-shaped, making a second curve around the poplar grove. Although the storm had knocked it down, new trees were springing up fast from the root system.

After the grove the logging road began. It climbed through several acres of stumps and half-burned slash where pines had once flourished. Dexter Lewis remembered the storm well, for he'd been working on the road crew at the time, and trees had blown down all over town.

Near the top of the hill, a cool, shady stretch of woodland still remained. Here the logging road widened in a spot that had been used by the logger for turning his machine. I'd thought of planting flowers on the uphill side, where a semicircle of young pines provided a ready-made backdrop. When I mentioned this to Dexter, he offered to build me a stone retaining wall, for he was sure to be digging up stones, and this would give him something to do with them. I thought a wall was a fine idea. I could plant purple and white creeping phlox and other trailing plants in the crannies.

An open, sunny area came next, where a number of pines lay strewn on the ground. They had fallen recently, perhaps weakened by the storm, and I wished I could do something with them. It seemed wasteful to leave them lying on the ground, especially when I thought of all the boards that could be cut from them, and the price of lumber.

I knew my grandfather would have come up with something ingenious and useful. One time after thinning his woods, he'd made a playhouse out of saplings for me and my cousins, knocking it together in a couple of hours. It was really just a framework, like a line drawing: an outline of walls, doorway, and roof. He gave us the job of gathering pine boughs and lashing them together to cover the roof and the walls, which kept us busy for a week. After that, playing in the house and making the repairs that were continually necessary occupied us for the rest of the summer.

Dexter returned the next morning with his machine and set to work. The first day was devoted to the meadow, and by late afternoon the new ditch had been cut and the S-curve of the path raised and graded. On his own initiative, Dexter retrieved an enormous, flat granite slab from an ancient barn foundation on our property and carried it over past the vegetable patch to lay it across the ditch. It made a perfect bridge and seemed an auspicious beginning to the path, uniting the old and the new. I even liked the spray of weathered, barn-red paint spattered across it during some long-ago painting project by people who were most likely dead.

Seeing the paint carried me back in an instant into my own past, to a day when I'd gone to see my grandparents' old place in the Catskills. The property had passed out of the family decades earlier and had gone through several changes of ownership until it was finally abandoned. I found the place completely derelict. The doors I'd run in and out of all day as a child, the windows through which I'd gazed on rainy days hoping for a rift in the clouds, had all been boarded up. Despite the boarding, the front door had been smashed open. The place looked dark and ominous.

I didn't try to go inside. I had no wish to see whatever filth had been left lying around, and anyway the flight of stairs leading to the door had collapsed.

I did go into the garage underneath the house. The entrance gaped like the mouth of a cave, for the overhead door, the kind you have to haul up by hand, had been left open. I walked down the short, sloping driveway and stepped inside. The air was cool and damp, as I remembered. I inhaled deeply, but detected no trace of the aromatic fragrance of vinegar, garlic, and dill from my grandmother's pickle barrels. My grandfather used to pick the cucumbers from his vegetable garden every few days—his vegetables were always lovingly tended, unlike mine—and my grandmother would wash them under the pump and drop them in the brine. When my cousins and I were little, we used to tiptoe into the garage and sneak pickles. My grandmother, who could be stern, hadn't seemed to mind. Somehow we never realized it was for us that she made them.

The smell of the brine had seemed pungent enough to soak into the walls permanently, but it hadn't.

The barrels were gone. So was my grandfather's workbench, which I'd been hoping I might find, since it had been fastened to the wall.

Nothing remained of my grandparents. It was as if they had never lived—as if the summers I had spent with them in this place had never existed.

Then I saw the splash of paint on the cement floor. It was gray but had once been white. I knelt and touched it, and a blisteringly hot summer day came back to me in a rush. I was wearing shorts and sandals and nothing else—no shirt, I was that young. My grandfather had retreated to the garage where it was cooler, and as usual I'd trailed after him. He did interesting things and would often let me help him. That day he was getting ready to paint a kitchen cabinet he'd made for my grandmother.

First he spread newspapers on the floor, carefully, for he was a strong believer in preparation. Then he pried open a can of white paint. I volunteered to stir it, something I'd done before. "No lumps!" I said, before he could get the words out.

He smiled. "Okay. No lumps! First rate!"

But the paint was old and had thickened on the bottom, and in my eagerness to get the lumps out I somehow managed to knock over the can.

I burst into tears.

"Sha, sha," he said. "A little paint—" He tried to wipe it up with a rag.

I could not stop crying. This was not long after my parents' divorce, and every little thing upset me.

"Sha, sha." He dropped the rag and, cupping my face in his hands, drew my head toward his chest and held it there until my sobs tapered off and I grew quiet.

Outside the ramshackle house, pale green spears like iris foliage caught my eye. I looked again—it was iris, all right. Somehow it had managed to survive in the midst of the choking weeds and matted turf that had once been somebody's flower bed. My grandfather's, or somebody who had come later? There was no way of knowing. I decided it didn't matter. I would take a piece of the iris with me, and plant it in Vermont as a palpable link with my childhood, evidence that I had indeed spent all those summers in this place.

Since I had no shovel, I clawed a clump out of the earth with my fingers, breaking my nails in the process. I carried it off by the leaves, like a rabbit by the ears.

I didn't get back to Vermont for a couple of days, but I didn't worry about the iris. Like a wandering Jew, it had come a long way already. It was a survivor.

So it has proved to be. The following year, and every year thereafter, it has bloomed in my perennial bed: a small, old-fashioned, freckled yellow iris with an auburn beard. Not exactly beautiful, but persistent as a memory.

Dexter Lewis came every day at seven to work on the path, and I spent a lot of time watching him. I followed him from place to place as I had followed my grandfather, while memories of childhood summers in the Catskills came back to me. Yes, there had been a path: it had led to the brook where we used to swim—wade, rather, for even in the deepest spots the water had only come up to the grown-ups' waists. When I was very young I used to run down there almost every day, crossing a field where wild strawberries grew and a wood that had seemed deep and wild—a child's perception, for the wood was a mere strip of trees through which the brook could be glimpsed from the field. Yet wild mountain laurel and columbine grew along the path, just as I remembered them; and, in the brook, minnows still darted through the shallows over the shining pebbles.

Dexter had warned me there wasn't much he could do about the land that had been hit hardest by the storm, at least not for what I was prepared to pay. He did what he could, though, smoothing some of the churned-up earth and pushing the brush piles further away, hiding them behind big stones when possible. This helped, but the land still looked unsightly. I would have to wait for new growth to hide the damage. Five years, he said, would make a big difference.

In fact, a thin veil of green was already spreading over the bare soil. A few wildflowers had made their appearance, along with clumps of white birch, the trunks of which are dull brown for several years until they shed their bark like baby teeth and emerge snowy and new. The birches were springing up where the soil had been well stirred, for their seeds need to be scarified before they will germinate. Small, delectable raspberries beckoned here and there on long, thorny canes. Wild filberts had sprouted and in time would put out their nuts, hidden inside fuzzy, green capsules growing in pairs.

The storm had not denuded the hillside completely. There had been a sparse understory of maples struggling to grow in the shade of the pines, and many of these remained. Their thin, whip-like trunks had bowed before the force of the wind, instead of breaking like the rigid trunks of the pines. Dexter Lewis steered his machine between these carefully, for the runty, misshapen maples were at least alive, although bent at ungainly angles. Perhaps they would never grow normally, but they were beginning to lift their heads and spread their crowns in the unaccustomed sunlight.

This part of the path, where the landscape was bleakest, might well turn out to be the most interesting. It offered a close-up view of the regeneration of the forest. My grandfather would have loved to watch it with me, for he took a keen interest in growing things. That we can no longer share with our beloved dead the things they would have enjoyed is one of the hard facts of life.

In less than two weeks, the job was done. Grass seed was planted on the path, and over it hay was scattered to provide protection.

A few days later, it rained—a gentle, day-long rain that bathed the seeds in moisture and soaked into the ground without washing them away. It rained again, and the grass began to grow. Before long, a ribbon of green curved up the hillside.

When the grass was several inches high, I took my first walk on the path. With me was my friend and neighbor, Tom Maclay. He had come over to cut my lawn, arriving unannounced, as usual, for he is the one who decides when my grass needs cutting. I may see his massive pickup truck parked in the driveway and him setting the planks in place so he can unload the riding mower. Or I may suddenly be jolted by the sound of the mower cutting through the pristine morning air. A moment later his fine, Roman profile, aging a little now, will sail past one of my windows, riding high. Tom is a Yankee in a sense that I, a flatlander, will never be. These distinctions are important in Vermont even unto the second generation, and Vermonters have a saying: "If a cat gives birth in the stove, they're kittens, not muffins."

In the years since Tom had designed and directed the construction of our pond, he'd become a vital part of our lives. By now he was involved in most of my projects around the place, tolerating my ignorance and trying patiently to educate me. I'd discussed the path with him, but he hadn't been involved in the construction. In fact he had stayed somewhat aloof, as if not wanting Dexter Lewis (whom he knew, as he knew everybody) to feel he was horning in.

Now that the job was done Tom felt free to critique it. The spatter of paint on the stone that bridged the ditch didn't enchant him as much as it did me—"Wasn't there a clean one?" Yet I still reserved the right to like it.

The ditch met with his approval, but when I said I planned to grow marsh plants in it, he pointed out that the topsoil had been removed and piled on the path. All that remained on the bottom of the ditch was the grayish clay subsoil. As soon as he said it, I realized that of course this was going to be a problem! How could I have overlooked it? Later I was to find myself planting in pailfuls of good soil that I would dump into pitiful little holes gouged out of the clay. Naturally, no self-respect-ing bog plant would grow under such conditions, and the only thing that flourished was turtlehead.

Partway up the hill, we encountered a wet spot on the path. "Spring," Tom said. "Better put in a piece of culvert. I've got one somewhere—I knew it would come in handy." He kept a vast collection of scrap metal and spare parts in his woods.

In a couple of places he said he would make a "water bar," which he explained was a depression across the path to keep water from scouring the surface during rainstorms and eroding the soil.

Aside from these few items, he declared the path a success, pronouncing it wide enough for him to maintain with his riding mower and not too steep. And he predicted a bumper crop of blackberries.

In the next few weeks I walked on the path often. My husband inspected it, after spraying himself liberally with OFF! to keep the mosquitoes at bay, and said it looked pretty good, except that the grass was thin. I assured him it would thicken as it grew. One or two friends came by and gave the path their seal of approval.

Mostly I was alone on the hill, planting. I tucked creeping phlox in the new retaining wall and columbines behind it. I longed to plant mountain laurel, but Vermont winters are just too cold. Instead I settled for the toughest locally-grown azaleas I could find. Even these came with no guarantee, for now and then a killer winter comes along. I wasn't exactly trying to reproduce the Catskill path of my childhood, but I wanted the columbines and azaleas to remind me of it, and of my grandfather.

Planting on the hill was difficult, for the never-cultivated soil was full of gnarly roots. Blackberry brambles and big, tough ferns were poised to invade the area I'd marked out for planting, and weeds sprang up everywhere in wild profusion. Worst of all, there was no source of water. I had to bring it up in buckets. This preyed on my mind, and I hunted around for a spring. I knew of several springs on the hill, one of which provided our house water, but all were lower down, and hence no help. A pump could have brought the water uphill, but it was more of a challenge to find a source of water that was independent of technology. Anyway, pumps tend to freeze and crack in the Vermont winter. I didn't need much water, for the rains were generally reliable; but when planting I had to have some. It would be enough to have a barrel filled with water for dipping, which the rains could replenish.

What I needed was a rain barrel. Probably not many people today have seen a rain barrel, although in the old days they were common. My grandfather had one, which was set under a downspout from the roof. Every time it rained, water poured into the barrel. Whenever he planted seedlings, or a tree or shrub, he used to dip up a pailful and pour the water carefully around the roots. He would keep doing this until the roots were well established. He had a hose, but it doesn't hurt to be sparing with your water in the country, especially during droughts.

Why couldn't I have a rain barrel? The answer was simple: no roof, no downspout. Just leaving a pail under the open sky wouldn't do the trick—I'd already tried that with a big trash can, and only a few inches of water had collected. I needed a roof. Why couldn't a hut be built from the fallen trees that were lying around?

I consulted Tom. He listened, white-thatched head cocked, and I could see his mind working. He is a born tinkerer, and like a true Yankee, thrifty by nature. He took the shovel I had been using, walked over to a pile of logs that Dexter Lewis had collected, and bent over and inspected the ends, to which he gave several hard pokes with the shovel. "Not too bad," was his verdict. "Sure, I could build something, get one of the boys to help me. Wouldn't cost you much. How big would you want it, do you think?"

"I don't know, maybe eight by eight. Small. Nothing fancy, just four posts and a roof."

"Better not be fancy, you want me to build it. No power up here. Guess I could use the chainsaw—"

And so it was decided. Tom would build a hut at the highest point of the path, next to the stone wall.

One bright fall morning when the maples were turning scarlet and gold, Tom and one of his grown sons arrived to start work on the hut. The sun had just cleared the ridge. Spider webs beaded with dew hung in the blackberry bushes, and on a patch of bare earth a deer had left its hoofprints. The air was crisp and cool.

The men would be building the hut with methods that were fairly primitive, for there was no electricity on the hill, and I was interested in seeing how they would do it. I settled down on a stump to watch, admiring the absolute authority with which Tom addressed himself to the task. He was no youngster, but he was strong and seemed to know exactly how to go about the job. As for his son, Timmy, a sturdy, good-looking man in his thirties, he was walking around inspecting the fallen trees. When he found one he liked, he stripped off the branches with his chainsaw, hoisted the trunk on his shoulder, and brought it over to the hut site.

Tom selected a long, straight log for the first post. We decided not to take the time to strip off the bark and coat the logs with preservative, or to build a stone or cement foundation; this was not to be a structure for the ages. We were using mostly found materials, and the hut, when finished, would blend almost invisibly into the forest as if part of it. The posts would decay in not too many years— for some reason this didn't bother me. Decay was inherent in the natural processes that would be going on all around it, and the hut would not be exempt.

Things that don't last forever can still be worthwhile. I had learned that lesson a long time ago, for hadn't I spent years doing things that were gone by the end of the day, when my children were young and I was a housewife? Had those pancake breakfasts, those sandwiches lovingly packed in paper bags, those neatly made beds, swept floors, piles of sweet-smelling, freshly-laundered clothing been pointless because evanescent? I'd been weaving the texture of our lives, making an orderly world in which my husband was cared for and my children could grow. On some level I'd always felt this. Smoothing sheets and baking banana bread had been creative acts, like those elaborate floor paintings women make out of flower petals in some parts of India, which are swept away when the sun goes down.

Tom set the log into the hole and held it upright while Timmy shoveled dirt around it. When the hole was half full, Tom stepped back and adjusted the log. Then he picked up his axe, holding it delicately by two fingers and letting it dangle head-down so that it could serve as a plumb-line. Rearing back his head, he squinted to see if the post was straight. When he judged it to be satisfactory, father and son packed dirt and stones into the hole, working together in a wordless harmony that was lovely to see.

Again I thought of my grandfather. Somehow he had become inextricably mixed with the path and the hut and everything around me. The woods themselves seemed to summon up his ghost.

I recalled a story he'd told me once, about something that had happened when he was eight years old. He'd been playing in the woods near the river Berozhina. Suddenly he heard a bell ringing, and a few minutes later he saw a procession coming toward him from the direction of the river. The Russian Orthodox priest from the church in the village was walking in front in his golden robes, swinging a bell. My grandfather hid behind a bush and watched as the procession passed. About a dozen men followed after the priest; they were carrying the body of a drowned man.

That was the end of the story. The incident had remained in his mind for sixty years, and it has stayed in mine for almost as long again. It is odd to think I may be the only person alive who knows—in a sense remembers—what happened that day. This is the power of a story and especially of a vivid detail, for it is the priest's golden robes, so mysteriously out of place in the woods, that fixed the story in my mind. That, and the fear I sensed in my grandfather, as if he were still that little Jewish boy.

The following day, Tom and his son attached the beams that tied the posts together, nailing them on with long spikes: four beams to support the floor, and four to hold up the roof. Each beam was a hefty pine log with the bark still attached.

Before the beams could be attached, it was necessary to make sure the shed would be perfectly square. They could have used a metal try-square, and I don't know why Tom hadn't brought one along; but he hadn't. Instead he cut a straight piece of twig about eight inches long. Then he took a length of string out of his pocket and laid it out on the ground. Starting at one end of the string, he carefully measured three twig-lengths and made a knot. Next, he measured four twig-lengths and made another knot.

And I was absolutely astounded. It was as if thinking about my grandfather had conjured him up in the flesh. I knew what Tom would do next, and he did it—measured five twig-lengths and made a third and final knot, just as my grandfather had showed me when I was a child. Just as he, himself, had learned to do when he was thirteen years old.

"A house, it should be square," my grandfather told me, as he hammered a stake into the ground to mark the corner of one of the many houses I remembered him building while I was growing up—I think that time it was my Aunt Ida's. "It shouldn't be crooked, the floor boards should meet nice, straight, it shouldn't go this way and that way, it shouldn't give you a headache if you look on it. A headache you wouldn't want, right?" And he leaned toward me, laughter in his eyes. He hadn't really been old then, although to me of course he'd seemed ancient, with his skin that was weathered and freckled from working outdoors, and his thick, yellow fingernails, one of which was sometimes blackened by a blow from his hammer. He clutched his bald head, which was covered by a cap stenciled with the name of the local lumberyard. "Oy, every time you take a step on the floor your head it hurts like anything! Ow! Ow! Ow!" He was squatting next to me looking into my eyes, seriously now. "So! How you going to make sure—positive!—your house it should come out straight? Hah? You don't know, hah? And when I was your age you think I knew? I didn't know nothing! I wasn't smart like you, always the nose in the book." But I knew very well that he was smart, and that he, too, liked to read, especially the novels of Jules Verne, even though he'd had to leave school when he was twelve years old. His widowed mother had needed his wages and had apprenticed him to a carpenter.

"So you want I should tell you a trick?" His voice had sunk to a confidential whisper. "You take a piece string, like this." He measured out three units and made a knot, then four, and then five, and connected the first and last knots. He shaped the string into a triangle with a knot at each corner. "See?" He indicated the angle between the shorter two sides. "Straight! Square! This you should remember, this you shouldn't forget." And tying string to the stake that he'd hammered into the ground, he squared up the corner of Aunt Ida's house.

My grandfather had shown me simply a 3-4-5 right triangle, which I later learned about in geometry class. To my unschooled grandfather, it was a trade secret that had been imparted to him in youth—perhaps in woods not unlike these—lore vital to his becoming able to practice his craft. He never lost his sense of wonder at the mystery of it, or stopped marveling at the amazing fact that the corner of a 3-4-5 triangle would come out square—every time!

✦

We built the path six years ago, enough time for me to report on how it has worked out.

First of all, I love it—even though I don't walk there as often as I thought I would, because I'm naturally lazy. It is wonderful at all seasons. The lupines I planted in the meadow have spread to become a sea of glorious blue in early summer. And there are innumerable other flowers to enjoy while walking on the path: daisies, black-eyed Susans, and blue-eyed grass; purple vetch, Queen Anne's lace, and red clover. Milkweed flowers fill the air with their hypnotic sweetness, and butterflies hover above blue New England asters. In late August the annual wave of goldenrod breaks over the field, signaling the end of summer.

The bare ground where the storm hit hardest has now been covered by growth that is endlessly interesting to see. The understory maples have filled out a bit, although they still look scrawny—probably always will, like adults who suffered from vitamin deficiencies as children. The balsam fir seedlings my son and daughter-in-law planted along one stretch of the path have grown into thrifty little trees, four to six feet high. Still, these have been much outstripped by the white pines that began to spring up several years after the storm, when we'd begun to despair of ever seeing pines on the hill again. Now young pines are everywhere and growing rapidly.

One of the birches has finally shed its dull brown bark. Now it shines like a bride in a slender, white dress. Hopefully the others will soon follow her example, until the ivory gleam of white birch, a tree I especially love, flickers everywhere through the returning woods.

I regret to say that the flowers I planted at the top of the hill haven't done too well, even though the pair of blue plastic rain barrels Tom rigged up for me—he was so pleased to find them on sale that I didn't have the heart to object to the color—worked out perfectly. But the deer ate the hosta shoots, and I have been very neglectful about weeding. The bed is too far from the house, and something always comes up that seems more pressing.

Nevertheless, although the unweeded and unfertilized azaleas are small, they do bloom. The creeping phlox may be weedy, but encountering it blooming on the stone wall in the spring—white, pink, lavender—is a lovely surprise. The columbines died. They got too much sun and not enough water. Mostly, the ferns have taken over. I guess worse things could happen.

It is quiet on the path, except when the wind stirs the leaves of the young trees. It is the kind of deep quiet that city dwellers and suburbanites never know. In Maryland, I can hear the roar of the Beltway all the time, although I live on a residential street that is considered quiet, in a house located at least a mile from those eight lanes of traffic. The sound is there at all hours, in the background, imperceptibly fraying the nerves of millions of people every day. It is the first thing I notice at six in the morning, when I step outside to pick up the newspaper. I can hear it inside the house, too, if I listen, even with the windows closed.

The sky above my Maryland house is noisy, for we live not far from three major airports and one smaller one. We often hear jet planes. Traffic control helicopters rattle the glass in our windows as they roar overhead during the rush hours on the Beltway—they call them "peak hours" now. I suppose these name changes are intended to disguise unpleasant realities, and a "peak," with its suggestion of aspiration and achievement, sounds more attractive than a "rush," a word that makes one's muscles tighten up. The peak hours seem to be expanding. In fact they have become so long in the morning and evening and during lunchtime, too, that they have pretty much merged. Perhaps this is to be expected, even hoped for, in a great commercial civilization like ours.

In our part of Vermont the skies are generally quiet, except for thunderstorms. But there are certain fine, clear days in midsummer when an annoying drone fills the air and a small airplane makes its appearance overhead. It passes and repasses, disappears beyond a ridge and reappears from another quarter of the sky. Our path seems to draw it like a magnet. It is the marijuana plane, checking for signs of this illegal crop, which everyone knows is not uncommonly grown in home patches, in old barns under artificial light, and sometimes in extensive fields in the Vermont hinterlands. Sometimes it is raised surreptitiously on state land, where the growers will be harder to identify. I've heard estimates that its contribution to the local economy makes it one of the state's biggest crops; but no one really knows, especially since Vermont's dirt roads have a way of petering out into rutted byways, and vague tracks threading into the woods, where large, unfriendly dogs and homesteaders carrying shotguns have been known to appear unexpectedly.

The marijuana plane starts patrolling in early summer, when the bright green shoots of the plant are developing nicely; but the annual raids, of which there are a few each year, don't occur until just before harvest time, although there seems to be no reason except sheer meanness why they can't take place earlier in the growing season. One or two of our friends become quite irate whenever the small plane passes overhead; I never ask them why.

The marijuana plane spends a fair amount of time checking out our path, like one of those drug-sniffing dogs in airports, and it returns several times during the summer, as if the pilot can't quite convince himself he hasn't missed something. Perhaps our path has become part of the pilot's invisible garden. Something about the width of the path, the care with which it is maintained, and the seemingly pointless way it climbs the hill, runs along the ridge where there aren't any houses, and drops down to return to the road may evoke certain associations in his mind—and I doubt they would be of blackberry picking, poetic rambles, and mild aerobics.

But that's the thing about invisible gardens. They're unpredictable, because they are carried around by individuals who bring to them their own unique store of memory and experience. When I made the path, my thoughts were earthbound. I never dreamed I might be forging a future relationship with the pilot of the marijuana plane, a person I will probably never meet. Still, I like to think our path has enriched his life a little, by presenting him with a puzzle, something to think about during the long Vermont winters, when boredom sets in and cabin fever becomes a problem.

The hut is still standing. It blends into the woods, and newcomers don't see it until they are right upon it, when it appears like a personal discovery. Four steps lead up to the door, because the hut is on the uphill side of the path, and inside I keep a green box of tools and three old chairs. "Old chairs" suggests something quaint and old-timey. Actually, they are aluminum lawn chairs with plastic webbing, which we brought up from our house in Maryland and stuck in the hut "temporarily." Two of the chairs are chaises lounges, and the third is a rocker. I generally sit in the rocker, because the chaises are the kind that are quite comfortable while you're in them but almost impossible to get out of.

I still intend to buy nice-looking chairs some day, but what's the rush? The hut is only going to collapse anyway, one of these days. In the meantime, it is one of the pleasantest places I know for a cozy, intimate conversation or a nap. Guests seem to love it, and often when I

bring them there they begin to speak of whatever is clos-
est to their hearts—or else they fall asleep. Screens keep
the bugs out, and this helps me lure my husband up
there occasionally, for he knows that on top of the hill he
will find respite from the swatting.

There is a sense of being suspended in an utterly private space, remote from the rest of the world, out in the
woods where you can watch the birds and squirrels yet
be hidden enough not to disturb them. I know deer are
nearby: I've seen their tracks although they seldom
show themselves. Bears have passed through the woods,
for I've found their scat on the path during blackberry
season. They are shy creatures, and I've never seen
them. Still, I keep an eye out when I go berry-picking. I
wouldn't want to come between a mother bear and
her cub.

I've never known such a place as our path for picking
blackberries. The bushes line long stretches on both sides,
and you can reach them easily from the path, without
being scratched by the thorns. Friends like to come over
to pick with us. Tom picks blackberries there once or
twice a summer and later brings me a jar of jam his wife
has made. Occasionally strangers pick, too—sometimes
they ask permission and sometimes they don't.

The abundance is almost heartbreaking. We pick and
pick until we are worn out and the sun is sinking over
the ridge, but how can we stop? There is always one
more bush where the berries hang thick and luscious—
big ones, beauties, just begging to be plucked. Later
there are the pies, heaped and mounded with berries,
and crowned with dollops of whipped cream. And there
are the pints and pints of jam (it would be a crime

against nature not to make jam), given away to friends or opened and eaten on toast in the middle of winter, when they bring back those magical hours on the hill, days we were baked by the sun as we stretched for the berries that were sure to be sweetest because they were just out of our reach.

A path is like a life. It rises and dips down again. One has a dream, one makes a plan. Some things work out as expected, and others come as a total surprise. Mistakes are made. One stumbles and falls—and has moments of glory. Character flaws and strengths become apparent and affect the outcome. Walking along the path, one is aware of the terrain nearby and just ahead, but loses sight of the big picture. Eventually one comes out not so very far from where one started—"in my end is my beginning."

I still have my nose in a book, and I still draw wisdom and strength from my grandfather, who loved to tell stories.

Little Houses

Last year when we came up to Vermont for the summer we found a note tacked to our kitchen door. I expected it to be from the neighbor up the road who had said she would leave groceries in our refrigerator, but instead it had been left by a stranger.

Hello!

You don't know me and I hope it's OK I'm leaving this note. I like your little house so much! I would love one for my girls 5 and 8. Could you tell me where you got it? I would appreciate it so much!

All the "i's" were dotted with little circles, and she had left her name and telephone number. This was the first time anyone had left such a note on my door, yet I wasn't really surprised. The "little house" that had caught her eye was our garden shed, and there is something about it that people can't resist.

Sooner or later, gardeners start thinking about sheds. We need a place to store the clutter: the rakes and shovels and hoes, the hand tools, the stakes and fertilizer and insecticide, the peatmoss and the lime, the twine and labels and baskets. We fantasize about shelves, lots of shelves. About bins and hooks and a proper potting bench where we can start seedlings in the spring, instead of crowding every windowsill in the house with yogurt cups full of dirt. About finally, once and for all, getting organized.

Often these dreams just drift around in the indefinite future. A potting shed costs money—how much is dauntingly unclear—and someone will have to build it. An amazing number of choices and decisions will have to be made, once one starts to get serious.

There are so many uses a small outbuilding could serve, and it is tempting to try and cram them all in. And then there is the important question of what the structure should look like.

I am not talking about the kind of sheds that farmers and mechanics build, which are necessary to their livelihood. I mean those less-than-essential yet persistent objects of our fantasies and desires, structures that are part of the invisible garden, sometimes because they don't actually exist and never will, other times because, although they are real and can be seen and touched, they have a meaning that transcends the obvious.

For some people, only a gazebo will do. It should be hexagonal or octagonal, open and airy, with a sufficiency of gingerbread and, if possible, a roof that comes to a point.

Gazebos conjure up visions of playing board games for long, lazy hours, of taking afternoon tea at a table covered with a white cloth while wearing a flowered chiffon dress (which will have to be added to one's wardrobe to supplement the usual pants and T-shirt); or perhaps of doing a spot of birdwatching, a pair of chased silver opera glasses in one's hand.

I know a mystery writer who owns a gazebo. She has an adoring fan club, and at a mystery conference the president confided to me with shining eyes that she had once visited her idol's home. "I saw her gazebo and everything," she told me, and then she fell silent. That seemed to say it all.

This particular writer turns out a prodigious number of books. She uses three pen names because her publisher feels readers won't buy three or four new books a year by the same author. She speaks casually of working twelve-hour days, "and then I fall off my chair." I don't see her spending much time in her gazebo, but apparently this is beside the point.

I went through a gazebo period myself. I bought a book that contained sketches of various gazebos and plans of how to build them. I saved a copy of a magazine that gave detailed instructions for the do-it-yourselfer. I even sent away for a catalogue to a company that shipped ready-to-build gazebo kits, all parts precut and hardware included. All of these provided me with many pleasant hours but never led to any action.

One day matters came to a head. My cousin Joyce, with whom I'd had gazebo discussions, called with a news flash. She'd heard that the owner of a house that had just gone on the market was interested in selling his gazebo separately. He would even truck it to the home of the purchaser. I didn't know the seller but I knew the gazebo, for I'd often admired it while driving down the road, even though it was the color of natural wood—not white, as I felt a gazebo ought to be.

It seemed this might be an opportunity. At the least it was an excuse to take a closer look at the gazebo and discover how it felt to look out instead of in.

I drove over a day or two later. The owner was eager to sell and named a price that seemed reasonable, though not irresistibly cheap, especially since I'd have to have someone build a foundation. He told me, "all you'd need to do is give it a coat of polyurethane every spring."

With these words the magic fled. An annual chore had played no part in my gazebo fantasies. Suddenly I became critical, though not aloud, for I didn't want to hurt his feelings. Why, the place was tiny—what could I possibly do with it? Two nasty little benches filled most of the space, leaving hardly any room to squeeze in a table. Through the open walls, mosquitoes and black flies brought me within their range finders, and dived. Scratching the bites on my arms, I shook my head and stepped out of the gazebo.

The roof didn't come to the right kind of point, either.

The owner sensed the shift in my mood. "Maybe you could use a covered bridge?" he asked, not very hopefully. A miniature specimen led to his front door, crossing nothing in particular. It was authentic in every detail, and exquisitely crafted. He'd made it himself, he told me. "No thank you," I said, for diminutive covered bridges were a species of "little house"—no wonder the English used to call them "follies"—that didn't interest me. Yet they must play a part in Yankee fantasy lives, for

I've noticed them here and there in Vermont, a state where real, functioning, covered bridges are still to be found.

I left, and so ended my interest in gazebos.

Since for some reason there are an inordinate number of writers in our part of Vermont, the writing cabin is a type of little house that comes up for discussion quite often. It is closer in spirit to the workaday potting shed than to the frivolous gazebo, yet has elements of both. The task at hand, writing, is uppermost (or should be), but there is also a certain mystique about the idea of the author's writing cabin at the far end of the garden, or tucked away in the woods, or overlooking the sea or Walden Pond. Writers are aware of this, even the most famous—they too were once aspirants shaping their conception of the writing life. "I'm going down to my writing cabin," they remark offhandedly, as if saying, "I'm going to the office." And in a sense that's all they're doing. But the writing cabin is also a shrine where the rites of invoking the muse are carried out and where, it is hoped, she will get into the neighborly habit of dropping by on a daily basis. Computer or no, writing is still a mysterious process. Most writers seem to think it takes some combination of inspiration and habitual effort—"just showing up," as Woody Allen used to say—but beyond that there is little agreement. Some writers seem able to sit down and begin as if flipping a switch. Others agonize—even the prolific Agatha Christie knew despair halfway through writing a book. Some thrive on sex, drugs, and rock and roll while others require silence, afternoon naps, and lives of dull routine. Some must be able to see the sky while they are writing, and others pull down all the shades if the weather outside is too perfect. Some go to Dionysian extremes, like Georges Simenon, who used to check into a hotel and binge-write a book in a few weeks, followed by sex in massive doses.

The important thing is to know the kind of writer one is, and to arrange one's life accordingly. Writing cabins and other writing spaces reflect this truth. Some are as bare as the cell of a monk, with all distractions pared away. Others are a clutter of books, maps, clippings, cartoons, stones, feathers, leaves, tacked-up quotations, and photographs, all of which may help stimulate the imagination.

One of my writer friends keeps trying to talk me into building a writing cabin, although since my husband and I are the only ones in the house, and sometimes for months I stay there alone, I don't usually feel the need for one. When I had children at home it was different, of course; and even now I can be distracted by domestic concerns, especially when we have house guests. I think women find such distractions more pressing than men do, although I'm not completely sure of this. In most societies women are more responsible for the things inside the house and men for the things outside, which explains why there are so many conflicts over taking out the garbage.

The fact is that my friend, even though she lives alone, wants a writing cabin herself, though she claims she can't afford one. The latter isn't true, for a small, simple structure would be within her means. The basic difficulty is that she can't make up her mind whether what she really wants is a writing cabin, or a little guest cabin where a grown child could stay during visits.

I understand this perfectly. It is the eternal problem of the writer who happens to be a mother. On the one hand we long to spend time with our cherished offspring, cook their favorite foods, listen when they want to tell us their troubles, go on outings with them, spoil them a little, and on the other we know in our bones that these things are incompatible with writing. Once that child is in our house, he or she will be on our minds, not to mention on the convertible sofa in the study, sleeping (quite possibly with a lover) as late as possible. Our writing will pay a heavy price, not only while the child is present but for days or weeks afterward, until the break in our routine can be repaired.

The reason my friend can't make up her mind whether she wants a writing cabin or a little guest house is that either one would do the trick. It doesn't matter which she picks. What she needs is to separate herself from her loved ones so that she can write and still have the feeling they're around. Once they go home she'll have the place to herself and can get on with her work without requiring a little house of any kind.

As my garden expanded, the need for a potting and storage space grew more pressing. But my budget was tight, and I was reluctant to hire a carpenter and build a little house from scratch. I was afraid I wouldn't be able to resist adding this and that, on the "as long as I'm doing it, might as well do it right" principle, and end up with something I couldn't afford. A cupola and a weathervane were already trying to attach themselves to the roof.

There was a lot to be said for buying a ready-made shed, if I could find one I liked. At least I would know the price from the start. But when I inspected the miniature barns and storage buildings and potting sheds lined up outside the nearest mega-hardware store, none of them seemed right. They were affordable, but I didn't care for the chipboard walls, the barn-like doors, and the absence of windows.

I'd heard that a young couple named Michael and Uli, who live up the road from us, had solved the little-house problem by finding a carpenter who built ten-by-twelve structures for a thousand dollars. These had a window and a regular door and were made of real wood, which the carpenter precut to standard lengths and brought to the customer's property, where he would put the house together, making any necessary adjustments on the spot. Michael and Uli had acquired one, so I asked if I could come over and see it. They graciously invited me to tea the next day, although they are busy people with not only two young children and a three-legged dog to keep them occupied but a successful business, which they run out of their home.

"Oh, we love little houses!" Uli said, as she poured tea into my cup. She is a small, slender person with large bright eyes and a German accent.

"Actually, we have two of them," Michael said, passing around a plate of low-fat cookies he had baked.

"Why do you love them?" I asked.

Uli's eyes grew dreamy. "Little houses are really intimate. They fit you like a piece of clothing. You know every pocket." To Uli, a designer of children's clothing, pockets are full of meaning, whether or not there is anything in them.

When the couple bought their old farmhouse, there were already two tiny, one-room cabins on the property, standing close together in a field at a considerable distance from the main house. Later these two little houses were joined into one by adding an enclosed entryway that linked them together. Now this cabin, still very small, is used as a guest cottage.

We walked down to see it. It was painted green and blended into the landscape. A short distance away, an old-fashioned outhouse was tucked discreetly behind a clump of bushes. "You go in here," Uli said, opening a door in the middle of the cabin. We followed her inside, completely filling the entryway. "And you can turn either left or right." The room on our left contained a bed, dresser, and storage cupboards, and the one on the right a doll-size kitchen, with a table and chair, a water spigot, a small sink, and a gas stove. The carpentry was crude, and there was no electricity. Both rooms had windows on three walls, with views of rough-mown fields, venerable sugar maples, and an old stone wall. "The windows become the pictures on the walls," said Uli. "And you can sweep the whole place out in a minute."

I felt an urge to move right in, as if by doing so I could leave behind all complications—bills to be paid, unanswered letters, papers to be sorted and filed, clothing to be mended and washed or given away, repairs to be made, telephone calls coming at inconvenient moments—and achieve some ultimate simplification of my life. To what end? I didn't ask myself that as, regretfully, I followed Michael and Uli out the door.

The second little house, the one that had been built by the thousand-dollar carpenter, was close to the main house, although hidden from view in a grove of trees. It had a different feel. The wood was new, the roof shingles tight, and the corners perfectly clean and square. Although the house was shaded by trees, the interior had a cheerful brightness because of the floor-to-ceiling window that had been let into one wall, and the smooth, Sheetrock walls painted a fresh white. The window and the Sheetrock had been extra, Uli said. There was an electric outlet and a gas heater, but no water or outhouse; the place, quite simply, was a totally private bedroom that was, as Uli said, an extension of the house, a place to put a spare guest.

I wouldn't need Sheetrock in a potting shed, I thought, but I did like the window. Yes, the thousand-dollar carpenter was definitely a possibility.

Most of the summer went by, and I hadn't called him. Then one night about ten o'clock, while I was reading in bed, the telephone rang. It was Michael. "I was out bicycling," he said. "I saw the cutest little house. It's for sale, and I think you should take a look at it." He'd seen it at a local sawmill in a town some miles away, and he told me how to find it.

It always amazes me how many small, private businesses are tucked away in the hills of Vermont. Upholsterers, hairdressing salons, bicycle shops, bakeries, lampshade stores, antique shops—the list could go on and on—are to be found on dirt roads, in homes, and barns. The first time we took our youngest son, then in his twenties, for a drive after we had bought our house, we stopped at a home bakery we happened upon and bought fragrant, freshly baked honey buns. As we ate the delectable treats in the car, he said Vermont reminded him of Hobbit-land in *The Lord of the Rings*. Of course the reality is that Vermont is a rural state with a depressed economy, where people need to use their ingenuity and skills to supplement their incomes; but I knew what he meant.

Privately owned sawmills can still be found in small towns, although nowhere near as many as once existed. They usually consist of a long, roofed, semi-open shed containing a big circular saw and other machines, where logs are sliced into rough-sawn boards that are sold locally.

The day after Michael called, I drove to the town he'd mentioned and found the sawmill without difficulty. Piles of weather-worn boards were stacked haphazardly around an open shed, with long grasses, Queen Anne's lace, and blue flowered chicory growing thickly between them. The place looked deserted—perhaps even abandoned. The little house stood out in front, near the road. As soon as I laid eyes on it I knew it was The One.

I got out of my car and went inside the sawmill. No one was around, and when I called, "Anybody here?" there was no response. So I walked over to the little house, which is what I'd wanted to do right away, only I'd felt I should ask permission.

It was a diminutive log cabin with a saltbox roof overhanging a tiny scrap of porch. It looked like a child's drawing, with a door in the middle and a small window on either side. I stepped up on the porch, pushed the door open, and went inside. Although I am short, my head cleared the door frame with only a couple of inches to spare. Once inside, I saw that there were two more windows, one in each end wall, making four in all. The place had a spicy, piney smell, like a cedar closet. The house was, in fact, made entirely of cedar except for the shingles on the roof. It should last very well—I could forget about polyurethane.

There was nothing to be seen inside but the structure of the house itself. It reminded me of something, but I didn't know what. I loved it. I felt right at home. I looked out of each of the four small windows, in turn. They were really just openings. I would tack screening over them, I decided, to keep the mosquitoes out.

And then I remembered. How could I have forgotten? At my grandparents' summer place in the Catskills there had been a well, around which my carpenter grandfather had built a little cabin—a bungalow, he called it—to protect the well and store the lawn furniture. This shrimp of a bungalow had a small porch, and on each side of the door a window, only these had been real glass windows with curtains sewed by my grandmother, and Venetian blinds with white wooden slats. The blinds were fixed in place and didn't work, for my grandfather had cut them down from an old pair and simply nailed them up, but when I was a child they had magic for me. They made the bungalow look as if someone lived there, a playmate I could visit whenever I wanted company. I was an only child, and sometimes lonely in the way a child can be when surrounded by adults who are going about their business. This imaginary friend became real to me, even though in a way I always knew her to be an aspect of myself, someone I would get to know better in the distant future.

I used to run in and out of the bungalow all day, and on rainy days when my grandmother wanted to rest, she would give me an umbrella and send me out there to play. I never minded. I would have liked to sleep there overnight, despite the spiders in the corners; but this was not allowed.

The little house at the sawmill wasn't exactly the same as the bungalow, for Grandpa's well-house had been made of white-painted clapboard, not logs, and its porch had two built-in benches where I used to play with my dolls. But the houses were about the same size, and both felt like a little girl's dream of the impossibly perfect playhouse.

I stepped outside on the porch of the little house and stood looking around as if expecting a visitor, perhaps myself at the age of six or seven. A cardboard "For Sale" sign was nailed to one of the porch posts, and I copied down the telephone number that had been scrawled on the sign in Magic Marker.

The house was resting, lightly it seemed, on four cinder blocks, one under each corner. I wished I could pick it up, slip it into the trunk of my car, and whisk it away.

When I got home I called the telephone number. No answer. I tried it later in the day—same thing. I called all week, early in the morning and late at night and all hours in between, but the phone just rang and rang. It was very frustrating. I was sure somebody else was going to buy that little house right out from under me. Perhaps they'd done so already.

After a week I couldn't stand it, and decided to return to the sawmill. If the little house was still there I would buy it—that is, if anyone was around. If not, I would knock on doors in the neighborhood until I got some information. I took my husband along as reinforcement.

The little house was still there, and we went inside. After looking out of each of the windows in turn, Joe said thoughtfully, "This is a cute house. It reminds me of Robinson Crusoe." He'd read the book as a boy, and had liked the part where Crusoe builds himself a house, after the box of tools miraculously floats ashore from the shipwrecked boat. "I always wanted a little house like that," he said. "Let's get it!"

Again the sawmill was deserted, so we knocked on the door of a nearby house. A burly man opened it. He said the little house belonged to his cousin, Jimmy, who had made it.

I said, "Do you know how we could get in touch with him? I've been calling all week and he doesn't answer."

"Calling?" He looked confused. "Jimmy doesn't have a phone."

"But there was a phone number on the 'For Sale' sign."

"Oh, that," he said. "That was just an old 'For Sale' sign he found in the barn." He seemed to think this perfectly reasonable. I thought of my grandmother, who came from a family of merchants and was herself a keen businesswoman. She would have shaken her head, aghast at such a way of doing business.

He gave us directions to Jimmy's house, which wasn't far away.

We found the house without any trouble. On the porch were four transparent trashbags filled with empty beer cans. Jimmy didn't seem to be around, so we left a note on the door and went home.

A few days later the phone rang. At last it was the elusive Jimmy! He said he'd gotten our note. He'd made the little house one day when he'd been sawing logs for six weeks straight and "just wanted to build something." He figured if he couldn't sell it he would use it for a sauna. We agreed on a price, and the following weekend he and his cousin brought it over on a logging truck and set it in place near our vegetable patch.

That was how we acquired our little house.

The first thing I did after we got it was to hunt down a pair of the narrowest window boxes I could find, suitable for a porch that was only two feet wide. I can't remember whether the bungalow of my childhood had window boxes or not. I suspect it did, because of the urgency with which I felt our little house had to have them.

I hung the window boxes under the two front windows and planted them with red impatiens and trailing vinca. Since the boxes happened to be green, I painted a small chair green to match.

I put this on the porch, too. Only then did I start thinking about building shelves and storing garden tools.

Little houses are a conduit to childhood—that is their charm and their magic. They connect us in a very direct and immediate way to a time when our eyes had only recently opened on the world and our senses were fresh and new; a time when we played at being grown-ups because mere adulthood shone with an extraordinary radiance and glamour.

I doubt very much that the pleasure of moving into even the most splendid new home can equal the thrill a child feels playing in an old refrigerator carton with a crude window and door cut into it with a box cutter by an obliging relative. Children can never resist a really large box. Apparently the inborn human tendency to seek shelter shows up at an early age; other animals need to seek out dens and caves, why not people as well? Little girls generally seem to start setting up housekeeping, while little boys defend forts and establish exclusive clubhouses; whether this is due to nature, nurture, or a combination of the two, I don't know.

Playhouses give children a sense of power and control. Different versions of adult life can be imagined and tried out there. Treasures can be kept in them, hidden away from the rest of the world. Playhouses are totally manageable; they can be whatever the child desires, without any of the drawbacks that appear later in life. Upkeep, maintenance, fuel, insurance—all the polyurethane of life—never have to enter the child's head. Responsibility, and what my children used to call "the big M"—Maturity—still lie in the future. No wonder the child in the refrigerator box feels pure joy.

Little houses are precious because they recall that feeling and allow us to experience it again, if only briefly. The everydayness of life keeps trying to smother joy, yet the capacity to feel it remains latent within us. That is where joy resides, not in a "little house," or a flower from the garden, or any other material object. These are just talismans. They are Rorschach blots. If you find one that works for you, make it a part of your life. Go out of your way to see it as often as possible.

Fred

Sometimes after the children leave the nest, one of them returns with a broken wing. That summer it was our youngest child, Nora. She had been travelling through Europe, in search or in flight, staying for a while at a Buddhist center and meditating with people who were kind and hard-working. She'd liked the place, and I don't know what went wrong; she didn't write much. But a call came at three in the morning from somewhere in France. "Mom? Dad? I'm by the side of the road, I don't know where I am and I don't have any money—"

When she came home she was pale and thin, as if she hadn't been eating right for some time. She looked worn out. The ivory skin, the gray-green eyes, the dark rippling hair, all were dulled as if by illness. Even her long, slender neck was bowed.

She spent the following summer with us in Vermont, and we all really tried. She bought a little bell—they'd had bells at the Buddhist center—and the three of us would sit on the porch and hold sessions where we rang the bell and took turns talking, so we could clear the air of whatever grievances had accumulated. Sometimes these sessions helped for a while, but often they led to bitter wrangling that went on and on, especially between Nora and me. We just couldn't get along, and this had been true for the ten years or so since she'd been sixteen.

I wanted desperately to help her, but I couldn't seem to do what she seemed to want, which was to sit with her for endless talk sessions in which we rehashed the past but never resolved anything—just grew more and more angry and frustrated with each other. We kept reaching out to each other, yet our fingertips would barely touch before they would slip apart again. One thing I could do that pleased her was to make her a mug of herbal tea when she woke up in the morning. She liked that. And when she went outside and plucked a sprig of mint for her cup from my mint patch, it felt to me like the only time in the day I was able to give her something she enjoyed. I felt glad I'd decided to plant the mint, despite its wandering ways. I'd sunk a ring of rusted iron from an old wood stove into the earth, to restrain it.

She didn't like me to garden. "You're always walking around the garden and checking up on it, seeing how the flowers are doing," she said to me. "But you never just sit down with me and check up on me, ask me how I'm feeling."

I didn't see things the way she did, of course. How she was feeling was uppermost in my mind, and in my husband's, too, and we checked on her all the time, or so we thought. But she was a leaky bucket that summer; none of our efforts could fill it. If I ever needed the garden, it was then.

One day I asked her if she wanted to plant a tree. I hoped it might cheer her up. "Maybe a flowering tree," I said—thinking she'd like something flowery and pretty—"an apple tree, a crabapple?" Not many flowering trees will grow in northern Vermont.

She considered this and finally agreed, so we drove to a small nursery not far off. On the way, she said, "I think I'll plant an oak."

"An oak?" I was taken aback. "I'm not sure they grow around here. Maples, yes—I doubt the nursery will even have an oak."

I tried to recall if I'd ever seen an oak in the neighborhood. Once or twice, maybe.

She looked irritated, and I could feel another big, silent conflict ballooning up between us. I tried to deflate it. "I just mean, the winters get so cold. No point in planting something that won't grow." It was no use. I could tell when she'd made up her mind. "Why an oak?" I said. I didn't care what kind of tree she planted. I just wanted to be sure it would live.

She shrugged. "Because that's what I want." She didn't say any more.

I was impressed that she wanted to plant an oak and, on the whole, pleased. An oak was a strong tree.

We reached the nursery, and among the rows of potted trees were two red oaks. We bought the larger one, which had a skinny trunk and a meager plume of leaves. The tree was too tall to stand upright in the car, so we opened a window and let the crown hang outside.

"Drive slowly so it doesn't get wind-whipped," the woman at the nursery cautioned us.

We set off for home at a crawl. We didn't talk much, but the atmosphere in the car was friendly—so much so that, when we passed a sign saying, "House for Sale," we decided to stop and take a look.

The owner showed us around. We told her that Nora might be moving to Vermont soon and would need a house. I was pretending, play-acting a scenario in which Nora was married with a house of her own and—who knows—maybe also a couple of kids. It was what I wanted for her—along with whatever else her heart desired. She lingered in the kitchen, running her hand along the smooth, wooden counter and commenting on the sunlight that poured in through the window. But we couldn't stay long. The tree was out in the car and we had to get it home.

The atmosphere in the car remained relaxed on the way back, but as soon as we arrived, tension flared up again. There was a difference of opinion as to where the oak should be planted. Nora wanted it close to the house, where it could be seen from the bedroom and the driveway. I thought it should be further away, because an oak can grow into a very big tree that darkens windows and works its way into foundations. And since it was my house and I would be the one actually living with the oak in the future, I thought I should have some say in the matter. To be honest, I thought I should have the final say.

I went into my room and lay down for a little rest. By the time I got up she had dug a hole. It was about fifteen feet from the north wall of the house. Practically under the eaves.

I went outside and looked at the hole while she watched me, defiant but a little nervous. "That's a big hole," I said. "Which is—good. How about putting in some manure and peat moss and fertilizer?"

"Okay." I could see she was relieved.

I went and got them, and we mixed them with the soil. She had taken my best shovel, so I used the other one.

Then we lugged over the oak and planted it, watering it plentifully and tamping down the soil around the rootball. We hammered a couple of stout stakes into the ground and tied the skinny trunk to them to protect the tree from the wind.

Joe came out and took a picture of us. In it, Nora is standing with her hand on the trunk of the oak, not smiling but showing a certain pride. I am a few steps behind her, one hand on my hip and the other resting on a shovel. My expression is bemused.

After the picture was taken, Nora gave the oak a pat and said, "This is Fred."

Very briefly, she smiled; and I glimpsed for a moment the child I'd once known.

Fred remained alive that summer but didn't grow. I kept it watered, remembering my grandfather, who had taught me the importance of watering a tree deeply the first year. Nora had been named after his wife, my grandmother, the powerful matriarch of an immigrant family. She had died the year before Nora's birth.

Despite all the watering and the tamping, Fred's grip on the earth remained weak. Sometimes after there had been a storm, a gap would develop between the thin trunk and the earth, as if the wind had loosened the tree in the ground. I would poke my fingers into the soil, which was dark and rich—too rich, maybe? Was that possible?—and press it back firmly against the trunk.

In the fall, after Nora had left Vermont to take a job, I planted six King Alfred daffodil bulbs under the oak. They were the biggest, cheeriest, brightest daffodils I knew—common, but guaranteed to grow.

Sure enough, next spring they bloomed, their trumpets blaring brassily above the still-muddy earth. Nothing sensitive or self-conscious about these babies. "I'm great!" they proclaimed. "Hey! Look at me!"

Fred, though, didn't look so good. Over the winter the stakes had worked themselves free and now the whip-like trunk was bowed low, as if the weight of the few timid leaves the tree had put forth were too much for it. The gap between the base of the trunk and the earth had reappeared.

I pushed the stakes back into the ground and tried to straighten the trunk, which resisted my efforts as if it just wanted to lie down and rest from the battering it had received all winter. I brought a chair and a hammer from the house, climbed on the chair, and hammered the stakes in deeply. Then I tore two strips from an old, soft bedsheet, wrapped them around the trunk so that the bark wouldn't be chafed, and straightened the trunk by pulling on the ends of the cloth as if they were the strings of an old-fashioned corset, the kind my grandmother used to wear. Once the tree was standing upright, I packed compost into the gap until the base of the trunk was again in close contact with the earth.

Nora didn't come to Vermont that summer but remained in Maryland, working. She seemed to be doing better, although she had her ups and downs. The three of us had lived together for a year now and it was hard to leave her; but, after all, she was a grown woman and we had our own lives to live. We thought of her often and kept in touch by telephone, and in the fall we left Vermont for Maryland earlier than usual.

Over the next two years, Fred elongated and put out a few more leaves, although its crown remained sparse. But the skinny trunk didn't seem to gain in girth or strength, and in the spring I would find it bending over, pulling the stakes out of the ground. Then I would take remedial action.

I kept a worried eye on Fred during its first few summers. It grew so close to the house that I could hardly help seeing it, and whenever I did I thought of Nora—not that she wouldn't have been on my mind anyway.

I planted a circle of flowering myrtle around the base of the oak, over the daffodils that had developed into six sturdy clumps. The first year or two the myrtle was attractive, but the grass grew into the rich soil so aggressively that I couldn't keep the myrtle weeded; it looked a mess.

I tore out the myrtle, and a strip of turf beyond it, and made a round planting bed, which I edged with bricks to

keep the grass from invading. Out of the middle rose
Fred, in all its feeble glory. The tree looked straight, but I
knew it wasn't, for in the spring when I would loosen the
ties the trunk would flop immediately. But the oak continued to grow taller, and in the fall its leaves turned a
pinkish red that seemed almost to glow when we turned
on the outside light at the north end of the house.

I planted annuals in the round bed, red nicotiana in
the middle and fibrous begonias around the edges. The
next year I tried New Guinea impatiens. I used more
fertilizer than usual, in the hope that it would give Fred's
roots a boost. I didn't know whether or not all this fussing would affect Fred's fate, but I couldn't think of anything else to do to help the tree along. Finally I planted
five hosta elegans in the round bed. The big, blue-green
leaves make one of the finest ground covers I know, but
the plant takes a few years to really get going. Obviously
Fred shared that trait. The hosta might encourage Fred,
if plants could become friends.

The next winter was a rough one, but we got through it.
It was later than usual that my husband and I returned
to Vermont, and I was afraid I'd missed seeing spring
come to the garden.

As we pulled into the driveway, I saw that a few daffodils were still blooming at the foot of the oak. And
then I cried out, "Oh, no!"

"What? What is it?"

"Fred is dead!"

"Dead? Oh, no!"

All the other trees had put out fresh, green leaves; but from Fred's branches, shriveled little black bundles dangled like sleeping bats.

We parked the car and hurried over to the oak to inspect it more closely. It showed no sign of new growth. I made myself reach out and touch one of the disgusting black bundles. The thing broke off in my hand, and felt slimy.

"It must have gotten a disease," I said.

"How are we going to tell Nora?"

"I don't know."

The death of Fred cast a pall over our first week as we went through the motions of unpacking. We put away the things we had brought and took out the things that had been stored. We baited traps for the mice we could hear gnawing on the insulation in the walls. When we spoke to Nora on the telephone we didn't mention Fred; nor did she ask. I'd tried to keep her informed about the tree, sending occasional snapshots of its slow progress. I couldn't tell whether or not she was interested, and I'd wondered if she cared about Fred. Perhaps, for her, it had become like an outgrown toy a child might play with now and then to humor her mother, not because she really wanted to. If this was the way she felt, telling her about Fred's demise would be easier.

Yet I had a hunch that, deep down, she cared about Fred and would blame me for not taking better care of it. I knew Fred's death was not my fault, yet I felt guilty. And frightened; what Nora needed now were messages of hope, not bad omens.

At the end of the week my knowledgeable friend and helper, Tom, dropped by the house.

"I'm really upset," I told him. "You know that little oak my daughter planted? It died, and I don't know how to tell her."

"Now wait a minute," he said. "Let's take a look at it."

We walked over to Fred and surveyed it. The last daffodil in the round bed had faded, and the spears of the hosta had pushed through the ground and begun to unfurl; but I saw no change in the tree itself.

"Well, I'd wait a while," Tom said. "We had a late frost and it must have killed the leaves. I wouldn't jump to conclusions. Sometimes they come back."

Amazingly, he was right. A second crop of leaves began to appear two weeks later. I could relax—Fred had survived.

For some reason I don't pretend to understand, Fred's near-death experience proved to be a turning point, as if some dormant chemical had been shocked into action. By the end of the following year, the trunk had thickened and grown strong. It stood up straight and resisted the winds, even without staking. The top filled out with a bountiful crop of healthy leaves, and when fall came their coloring was exquisite.

I stopped worrying about Fred. It became simply my favorite tree.

One fall, a couple of years later, I decided to spend my first winter in Vermont. I knew I would need a garage, for I had passed the age when cleaning snow off a car every day was merely a minor inconvenience. The most obvious and best place to build one was the north side of the house, which faced the driveway. There was only one problem: Fred grew right in the middle of what I soon began thinking of as "the garage site." Fred, still Nora's tree even if she wasn't interested in it at the moment. Fred, which was finally thriving. I had known the tree shouldn't be planted so close to the house, and against my better judgment I had caved in, settling for peace in the here-and-now at the price of trouble in the future. Now the future had arrived, and much as I hated the idea, Fred would have to be moved.

It would have to be done quickly. The garage had to be planned, the contractor lined up, and the foundation dug as soon as possible, so that cement could be poured before freezing weather set in. I had never tried to transplant a tree, but I'd heard that autumn was a good time to do it. Not too late; the roots would need time to settle in before the winter.

I called a contractor, and he lined up a backhoe operator. As with any construction project there were scheduling delays, and snow fell twice before the backhoe arrived. The snow melted, but soon the temperature would drop to zero and keep on dropping.

I had picked a new location for Fred, halfway down the slope that led from the house to the pond. There the tree would be visible from the porch yet would not block the view. I might build a low stone retaining wall around it on the downhill side, to serve as a seat overlooking the pond. But this would be a project for the future.

That is, if Fred survived.

One cold, gray morning the contractor, the backhoe operator, and I went into a huddle. When I mentioned that my daughter had planted the tree, both men nodded; they, too, had children. Darryl, the backhoe operator, was to lift the tree with the scoop, securing as large a rootball as possible. David, the contractor, would be standing by with a shovel to dig out any roots that extended beyond the ball. The men would try to get all the roots, but if any broke off I would clip them. A clean cut would discourage infection.

Darryl, an old-time Vermonter, understood the importance of roots. He climbed into the cab of the backhoe and started it up. As he shifted gears on the big machine and worked his levers back and forth, the rusty teeth of the scoop nibbled into the soil with amazing delicacy. Fred began to tremble. Then it tilted. The scoop bit deeply into the earth, and Fred rose a foot in the air. Dirt crumbled away, revealing several long, thick roots that stuck out beyond the ball, still anchoring it to the ground. Darryl pulled on a lever, and the scoop shuddered to a halt.

David dug around the roots with the shovel and freed them. Darryl nudged the lever, and the oak rose a little higher. More roots. More shoveling.

There was a final lift, and with it a loud snap. A taproot concealed beneath the ball had broken. Praying that the damage wasn't crucial, I bent over, grasped the dangling stub, and made a clean cut.

The rest of the job was uneventful. By the time Fred had been moved to its new location, snow was falling. The men returned to the house to start on the foundation. I spread the exposed roots into comfortable positions and covered them with dirt, which I tucked snugly around them. Several clumps of daffodil bulbs had fallen out of the rootball. I retrieved them, separated the bulbs, and replanted them at the base of the tree.

Except for the taproot, the damage to Fred's roots had been minimal. How the tree would weather the winter still remained to be seen, but I felt hopeful. I tied the trunk to a couple of strong stakes, and even though snow was beginning to accumulate, I gave the roots a deep soaking. Once the ground froze, there would be no more drinks. Fred would be on its own.

The following spring, right on schedule, the oak leafed out as if nothing had happened. Only then was I able to tell Nora about the move. She was surprised. Why hadn't I told her sooner?

"I couldn't bring myself to do it," I said.

She said the new location sounded too far from the house, too exposed.

I told her I thought the tree would be fine. Then I said, "Why did you want to plant an oak?"

"Oh—I was just back from Europe. In Buddhism they talk a lot about having faith that even the smallest seed can grow into something magnificent. I wanted a tree that could survive a lot of harsh weather. I've always liked oaks because they're strong, enduring trees."

"I thought you'd want to plant a flowering tree," I said.

"That just shows how much you know me."

That summer, we built a low retaining wall at the base of the oak. It enclosed a small planting bed. In the bed, to form a pool of blue under the daffodils, I planted forget-me-nots.

Recently I told my daughter I was writing about Fred and asked her to tell me how she felt about the tree. She said, "It's your piece, so what you'll say won't be my statement. It'll be filtered through your words and your perceptions. It's your side of the story, it's not my side of the story. So you write it and then, if I need to, I'll have a rebuttal."

The Spring

The spring had been seeping out of the ground for a long time—how long, nobody knew. Generations, maybe, or centuries, or even millennia. It made its presence known by a muddy slope in a grove of ancient cedars, and a round, dark, persistent puddle in which a black salamander could from time to time be glimpsed.

From the moment I noticed the spring I felt drawn to it. It seemed to need a garden around it, a garden that was serene and contemplative, even spiritual; a garden that was enclosed yet half wild. I was vague about the details, for the conception that had come to me was more a feeling than a picture.

There was no hurry. Garden work near the house had to be tended to first. The spring was some distance away, on the far side of the pond. Still, every now and then for some years I tucked a few plants into the mud near the spring—primroses and astilbes, cardinal flowers and bleeding heart, plants that loved moisture and shade.

Now there were flowers near the spring; but they hadn't coalesced into a garden, certainly not the garden of my imagination. First it would be necessary to enlarge and deepen the muddy puddle, so that the water seeping out of the ground would collect and spread out into a small pool that could be seen from the path. A frame of some sort was needed, to keep the bright, brambly hillside from overwhelming the eye.

One Wednesday in August it suddenly became imperative to enlarge the spring-pool—why, I really can't say. Maybe it was a case of "self-organized criticality," to use the term of Per Bak, a physicist who studied sandpiles. He noticed that a sandpile that has been built up grain by grain will finally reach a critical angle and collapse in an avalanche; he then formed a theory that many important events, like the avalanche, occur in spurts, not gradually as had been supposed.

Maybe my "sandpile" had been the flowers. I'd dotted in an astilbe here and there until there were dozens, a primrose here and there until there must have been a hundred—more, if you counted the seedlings. I'd planted maidenhair fern, clumps of ginger, a white birch, hosta, and turtlehead.

Or maybe the sandpile had been composed, not of tangible things like plants, but of a certain kind of experience I'd had once too often. For despite all the flowers I'd planted, every time I'd gone by, my eye had slid right past them, past the spring, to the hill where the storm had leveled the woods six years earlier. Now blackberries rioted and wild cherries reached for the sky, battling the poplars for lebensraum, and a million leaves fluttered wildly, flashing in the sunlight like pennants strung up above a used-car lot.

I'd had to remind myself firmly, "There's a garden here, so look at it! This is a magical spot, dammit!" And by an act of will I'd had to refocus my eyes.

The day after the collapse of my "sandpile," Tom drove up in his truck. I hadn't been expecting him. I never knew when he was coming, for he was a busy man and fitted us into chinks in his schedule.

From behind the bedroom curtain I watched him unload the riding mower. He fired it up, and for the next hour the drone of the motor followed me around the house as I did my chores. Then I laced up my boots and went outside, waving to Tom as he steered the tractor down the grassy path to the meadow. He raised an arm in greeting but kept going. I headed in the opposite direction, toward the woods. I wanted to take another look at the spring before discussing it with Tom.

The spring looked just as usual, seeping out of the earth in the cedar grove a little way up the hill. The water in the puddle was of a limpid clarity and appeared utterly still. Nevertheless, somewhere a hidden current of water had to be flowing. It had carved out a shallow ravine that led downhill and was always wet.

Usually when I visited the spring, a sense of inner peace came over me. Not today, though. Today was strictly business.

Frowning, I surveyed the area. On the far side of the

small ravine, in the shade, the fluffy plumes of the late pink astilbes swayed back and forth like oriental fans, and Japanese primroses that had finished blooming were holding aloft their candelabras of dark brown seeds. Plump, emerald-green cushions of moss had swelled up here and there, and the feathery bed of wild lady's fern was thriving.

But the area closer to the spring was a mess. Here, in the sunlight, a tangle of brambles and weedy grasses had taken over.

And there was The Stump.

The Stump was big. It was ugly. And it was in the way. Before the spring could be enlarged, The Stump would have to go.

The stump explained the weeds. At some time or other one of the cedars in the grove had fallen, letting in the light that had caused the vegetation near the spring to explode.

I'd had my eye on the stump for several years, hoping it would rot enough to be pulled out without too much trouble. But cedar doesn't rot in a hurry. Unlike most kinds of wood, it withstands moisture and long contact with the earth. That's why it makes good fence posts.

Bending over the stump, I got a grip on it and tried pushing, to see if I could wiggle it. It didn't budge.

I straightened up, sighing.

I started thinking about backhoes. About bulldozers. About big money, and big, unsightly tire tracks all over the ground.

Discouraged, I headed back to the house. Tom was mowing at the foot of the lawn, sitting erect as he putt-putted along, the breeze ruffling his silver hair. His waist was a little thicker now than when I'd first made his acquaintance eight years earlier, but he was still a handsome man.

I waved, he waved back, and I went in the house.

A while later there came a tap at my kitchen door. Tom stood on the porch, his shirt speckled with grass clippings.

"Come on in," I said. "Have a seat, I'd like to consult you about something." He wiped his boots on the mat, and we walked the few feet to the kitchen table and sat down.

For the first five years after he started to work for me, Tom entered my house only once that I can recall. All the other times, when I asked him in he would shake his head with a dismissive wave that seemed to mean he was too wet, or sweaty, or muddy, or had no time for socializing, and anyway there was no reason we couldn't conduct our business right there where we stood, I on one side of the threshold and he on the other. The one time he did come in, it was because I'd asked him where I could get a new lock for the kitchen door, and he'd said, "Cost you money. Maybe I can fix it." I'd found a screwdriver, and he'd taken the lock off the door and sat down at the table to fiddle with it, the gleam of the fanatical tinkerer in his eye.

"Who mows your lawn?" a friend of mine once asked, and when I told her it was Tom she raised her eyebrows. "Such a fancy person?"

Fancy he was. Of course he knew the answers to all the questions I, a flatlander, and a summer person to boot, was always needing to ask of a local. Not only was

Tom a Yankee, he was his town's forest fire marshal as well as a member of the Board of Selectmen. He knew all the things that farmers know, for he'd farmed until the crawler had rolled over on him and broken his pelvis so badly he was in the hospital for eleven weeks.

When I first knew him he was holding down a government job that allowed him to get out in the field, which he loved, but also required more desk work than he really cared for. I owed the fact that he was willing to cut my grass to the fact that he had an expensive hobby—old cars. He liked to buy them, and pick up old parts, and swap and recondition them. His woods were full of them, he said.

He had an almost religious belief in the sanctity and dignity of labor. Chopping wood, cleaning houses, raking leaves, drawing up the budget for a government agency—some of it might be more enjoyable and some less, but it was all work and, hence, good. When he retired from his government job he kept right on working at various projects—his services were in great demand—and soon was busier than ever.

As the years passed, the stiffness between us gradually loosened up. Sometimes when I made jam I gave him a jar. Sometimes when he finished sugaring he brought me a can of maple syrup.

At first he just mowed my grass. Then he built me a bridge across a ditch and then a few other things. Summer by summer, we took each other's measure. Our lives and histories were very different. He'd always lived in the country and I came from the world of cities and suburbs. He was a conservative Republican, I was a bleeding-heart liberal. He was a Christian and I a Jew. He worked all day, and I took afternoon naps.

But we liked walking the land together, discussing this possible project and that. Some of these we carried out, with varying degrees of success. We settled into a comfortable collaboration.

Tom was already acquainted with the Stump, and he didn't think a bulldozer would be necessary. "Let's see if I can get it out with my come-along," he said. "I've got it in the truck."

The "come-along," as I'd already had occasion to learn, was a simple but effective ratchet device consisting of a lever, a metal box, and a length of chain. Loggers and country people still use these venerable tools when they need to move heavy objects.

Tom fetched the come-along, and we headed out to the spring. The massive, iron chain was dark with rust and looked heavy. "Haven't used this in a while," he said.

When we reached the cedar grove, he dropped the come-along on the ground. Then he walked around the stump, looking thoughtful, and jabbed it in a couple of places with the point of his penknife. He shook his head.

Shrugging, he picked up one end of the chain and walked with it to a tree some distance from the spring, where he secured the chain around the trunk. Then he walked back to the stump and looped the other end of the chain around it.

When he'd set up the come-along to his satisfaction, he began to pump on the handle.

Slowly the chain grew taut. As he worked the handle,

thrusting it down with all his weight, the chain tightened and started to cut into the wood of the stump.

He kept pumping, pausing frequently to catch his breath. "Not like when I was younger," he gasped.

It wasn't like him to complain. Watching him, I began to regret that I'd brought up the subject of the stump. I'd long taken for granted that Tom could do anything he set his mind to. His back had given him trouble ever since the accident with the crawler, but he refused to let mere pain slow him down.

"Tom—" I said.

He labored over the handle, breathing hard.

The pauses grew longer. The stump hadn't budged. He mopped his face and said, "Whew! Wouldn't want to do this for a living."

I said, "Maybe—"

I didn't know how to tell him to stop, without hurting his feelings.

He pumped the handle some more. The stump tilted slightly.

"Ha!" he grunted. "She's comin'!"

After that, the pumping went a little faster.

Finally, with a tearing sound, the stump keeled over on its side.

He straightened up, rubbing his back. Then he went over to the stump, and with a few strategic blows of his ax, severed the last roots. He rested a while, catching his breath. Next he squatted behind the stump and tried to shove it out of the way. I ran to help, and we pushed until the stump flipped over. Shoulder to shoulder we managed to roll it into the underbrush.

Water began to ooze into the hollow the stump had left in the ground. Tom said. "Guess it wouldn't hurt to dig it out a little."

"You mean today?"

"Could," he said.

"Aren't you tired?"

"I'm fine. You'd need a dam."

"Couple of logs?"

"Couple, three. Pack 'em in with clay. Got any cedar?"

"I don't think so."

He pondered. "Wait, didn't we leave a couple of logs behind the vegetable garden?"

"Now that you mention it, yes!"

We looked at each other.

He grinned. "Might as well get it over with."

We took a break for lunch. I invited him to join us in the kitchen, but as always he refused politely, preferring to sit in his truck and eat the lunch he'd brought along. After half an hour I saw him go by my window, carrying one of the cedar logs from the vegetable garden. The log was balanced on his shoulder, and he was steadying it with one hand. In a few minutes he returned for a second log, and then a third.

The logs were about twelve feet long. Tom smoothed them with his chainsaw to make a tight fit. Then he laid them across the ditch below the spring and buried the ends in the banks. He braced the front of the logs with heavy stones. Now it was time for the serious digging to begin.

He dug methodically, thrusting the spade into the muddy soil and tossing the clods against the back of the

logs. Pausing, he said he thought it wouldn't hurt to re-
inforce the dam with a sheet of plastic. It wouldn't show,
he assured me.

I ran back to the house and hunted around the attic
until I found a thick plastic bag that had once contained
a mattress. I carried it out to the spring, where Tom had
cut a trench about a foot deep and started to dig a new
row next to it.

He inspected the plastic and said, "It'll do."

While he held the bag taut I cut it open, and then we
laid it against the back of the dam. I smoothed the plastic into place, working out the bubbles of air with my
hands as Tom flung dirt on top. Soon he hit a vein of
good clay, which he packed firmly against the dam,
stomping it into place with his feet.

After a while the plastic could no longer be seen, and
a shallow basin had been roughed in.

He dug out some primroses and irises that were in his
way, and I moved them to a moist spot lower down the
ravine. Then I weeded the astilbes, as well as an exquisite clump of starry moss I'd never noticed before. Tom
kept digging. Two big stones were sticking out of the
ground, but we decided it would be better not to remove
them. Instead Tom dug up to them and partway around,
forming an inlet. He christened the stones "the Straits of
Gibraltar."

Finally he climbed out of the hollow. Leaning on the
shovel, he surveyed his work for several minutes. "Should
fill by tomorrow," he announced in a satisfied tone.

The next morning I headed for the cedar grove as
soon as I got out of bed. Dew still lay on the grass, and
by the time I reached the woods the hem of my night-

gown was soaked. I peered through the morning mist, spider threads sliding down my cheeks.

It had filled! Water had risen to the top of the basin and spread beyond the Straits of Gibraltar. Now the two big stones faced each other across a couple of feet of water, guarding the entrance to a miniature bay.

The pool itself was about ten feet in diameter—small, as befitted a woodland spring, but big enough now to make an impact. The water had submerged some of the primroses, and I would have to move them. Also the surface of the water had a slightly oily sheen, from the disturbed earth. I thought this would pass in time. Otherwise the pool looked perfect, or would as soon as a few good rains had washed the splashes of mud off the rocks.

A few days later I went to the local pet store and brought home a dozen goldfish. They were plain and in-expensive ones, for they were to serve as an experiment. Could they survive in the woods, or would they fall prey to raccoons and birds? I emptied the tiny fish out of their plastic bag into the pool and watched as they headed straight for the spot where the spring emerged from the ground. There they disappeared under a clump of fallen leaves. A good sign, I thought. Even though they'd spent their lives in an aquarium until now, they seemed to have innate survival skills.

Twice a day I walked out to the spring to feed the fish, as the young woman who'd sold them to me had in-structed. It didn't feel like a chore, but a pleasure to which I began to look forward. Whenever I visited the spring I fell into a meditative state in which I stared down into the water and thought about nothing. Or I counted the fish, over and over, as they slowly and warily made their appearance and began to nibble at the food. The water was so clear I could see every pebble on the bottom.

Occasionally I talked to the spring. Why not? There was no one around to hear me but the fish. If I was becoming a bit eccentric in my old age, I figured I could handle it. "Spirit of the Spring," I would begin. It felt like the right form of address. Then I would give thanks for something that had made me feel good, or ask for strength to face a problem that had come my way. I kept my remarks brief; explanations didn't seem necessary.

One evening a beloved, elderly friend came to dinner. She was having chest pains, she said—some kind of spasm. No, no, she didn't need a trip to the emergency room; she'd had the same pain once before, long ago. I gave her a hot water bottle and a cup of tea, both of which she appreciated. But the pain didn't go away.

I'd told her about the spring and she wanted to see it, so after dinner we walked out there, very slowly. She kept touching her chest with her hand. While we were walking back, I noticed she'd stopped touching her chest.

Oh yes, she said when I mentioned it. The pain was gone.

It didn't recur for the rest of the visit, and when I called the next day she said she felt fine.

"Hmm," I thought. "What is it with this spring?"

When I'd hung up the phone I went out to the spring and tossed a little more fish-food than usual on the water.

It didn't seem like quite enough of a gesture, so I bowed my head and said, "Thank you, Spirit of the Spring." That felt about right. I stood there, motionless, until the fish came out of their hiding places and nibbled my offering as I watched.

Not that I believed in ritual, but I didn't see how it could hurt.

I still have plans for making a garden around the spring, a real one with miniature winding paths and stepping stones, some sort of enclosure, and perhaps a rustic shelter with a seat. I haven't gotten around to it yet, but it's been on my mind for several years. Maybe I'll do something about it—but maybe I won't. Lately I seem to find myself wondering if it isn't time for me to stop making gardens. Maybe I should even start cutting back on the ones I already have. This seems a reasonable idea at my age, for weight keeps creeping up on me, and I tire more easily than I used to. But when the ground begins to thaw and the smell of spring fills the air, I want to get my hands dirty. I feel that I still have a few gardens left in me. I might as well keep making them as long as I can.

Epilogue

The stream still flows through our land, looking much the same as it did when I first saw it. Trout can still be glimpsed near the dam, thriving in the highly oxygenated pool under the waterfall where nobody tries to catch them. More willows and brambles and birch saplings have sprung up on the banks, and weeds have grown through the mesh seat of the metal chair I dragged down there fifteen years ago.

A few more stones have fallen out of the dam. The waterfall gushes through the holes now, as well as over the top. One day the whole dam will slump into the pool below it. This won't be a catastrophic event, for although there was once a pond behind the dam, it had silted up before we came to Vermont; there's no big, impounded volume of water poised to sweep downstream and do harm to our neighbors. The water will simply run down a slope instead of over the dam.

I get down to the stream maybe two or three times a summer—I always seem to be busy with other things nowadays—but I still hear the rushing of the water when I open my window, and whenever I walk out the door I raise my head for a moment and listen.

I no longer feel guilty about the stream, or rather about the garden I used to think I would create along its banks. I've come to terms with the unplanted irises, unbuilt gazebos, and unlaid paths that used to nag at me as I drifted off to sleep. Once in a while a stray thought comes—"I could really do a little clearing along the streambank, just spend a few days, it wouldn't be that hard"—but then I remind myself that, yes, it would be hard, and I'm involved in enough projects already.

I seem to have made peace with my own limitations. Being in close contact with nature has had a lot to do with it. I find it steadying to feel myself a part of something so much grander than myself, something that keeps turning out sunsets and thunderstorms and moose and wild raspberries without needing the least help from me, something that nevertheless includes me in its warm, impersonal embrace.

I seem to have accepted, finally, that there is a finite amount of strength, energy, and self-discipline at my disposal, a finite amount of money in the checking account, and a limit to the number of hours in a day. I honor the choices I make, most of them far from heroic, such as that I might rather take a nap or do the crossword puzzle with my husband than clear the brush from a muddy streambank. Yes, I honor even my character flaws, which I now see as just an inevitable part of being human. I will always take on more than I can do, and do an imperfect job, and sometimes disappoint people; and I will never lose a significant amount of weight and become nimble and agile and tireless in the garden. Yet although I've grown less impatient and driven, I'm also aware that I could revert, if the right project came along and blindsided me.

The magic I first perceived in the stream was no illusion, not for me, and my impulsive decision to buy it has brought me the purest and most sustained joy I've ever experienced, even if things didn't work out exactly as I expected. Those first bright fantasies of presiding, like a Chinese poet, over a stream garden where I would spend all my time in writing and contemplation—perhaps in a fanciful pavilion—were like the dreams of youth: based on romantic ideas about country life and my own capabilities.

The reality turned out to be more mixed. Eventually I did make gardens, but closer to the house where I could reach them with the hose, and we could see them every day, and I could more easily keep the slugs and moles in check. I wrote, but not out-of-doors as I'd seen myself doing; I found I was better off inside, where there were fewer distractions, fewer bugs, and less glare on the computer screen. And I never got as much writing done as I thought I would or should, because I let myself be tempted by other things I also wanted to do. As for contemplation, I fell into it at odd moments when I wasn't meeting friends at the café for pizza, or playing hilariously bad bridge on the porch, or conferring with the plumber about the septic tank, or planning new projects with Tom.

Those early fantasies have so much power. They seem utterly reasonable and within our reach when we are still too inexperienced to have anything to compare them with. We don't yet realize how arbitrary they are, or that they are only based on versions of reality that happen to have reached us through the lens of a particular culture at a certain moment in history, and that our dreams and aspirations would be very different if we had grown up in another place and time. We absorb the ideas of a parent, or a preacher in a pulpit, or the author of a book we've read, or the director of a movie that has influenced us, unaware that they consist in large part of wishful thinking, repression of unwelcome realities, and sheer inventiveness. We spend our lives trying to reconcile our belief systems with the very different things we actually experience.

Spending time in the natural world helps. Nature has its own laws, some stern and some gentle; these reveal themselves if we are patient and willing to learn, and perceiving them brings us satisfaction and a measure of peace.

I once read somewhere that most gardens will disappear within three or four years after the gardener ceases to tend them. This idea haunts me as I grow older. I sometimes think of it at particularly trying moments, such as when the raspberry canes slash my arms and draw blood, or when I wrestle with a large stone, or when I teeter on the edge of a gully trying to yank out a weed that is my only means of support. "Why am I doing this?" I ask myself. "It'll all be gone as soon as I'm dead." Then I remind myself that this is true of most human endeavors, and I go on gardening.